SpringerBriefs in Law

More information about this series at http://www.springer.com/series/10164

Jan M. Broekman · Frank Fleerackers

Legal Thoughts Convert

Rethinking Legal Thinking

Springer

Jan M. Broekman
Faculty of Law
KU Leuven
Leuven, Belgium

Frank Fleerackers
Faculty of Law
KU Leuven
Leuven, Belgium

ISSN 2192-855X ISSN 2192-8568 (electronic)
SpringerBriefs in Law
ISBN 978-3-030-43516-5 ISBN 978-3-030-43517-2 (eBook)
https://doi.org/10.1007/978-3-030-43517-2

This Springer imprint is published by the registered company Springer Nature Switzerland AG
The registered company address is: Gewerbestrasse 11, 6330 Cham, Switzerland

Preface

"Law no longer practiced but only studied, is the gateway to justice."

Walter Benjamin 1934 on Franz Kafka's tenth date of death

This book highlights how *information* is one of the most important issues of legal thinking, not to mention legal practices all around. One of the major connections, which information needs, is a link with language. Texts in law, judgments, opinions, master ideas were always a matter of language, and because of that important position, information is connected with all varieties of linguistic forms and prescripts, but also with all social positions in law, like the traditional Civil Law sub-discipline expressed in analog language with the name "legal dogmatic". Inner forms of law and legal expression were ultimately the powerful modes of law's architecture and practice. But information is a complex concept.

It contains precious human values like communication, connection, mutual understanding, contact, desire to master the different, but also recognition of the otherness of the other and ultimately one's own identity amidst other participants in social life. Are such strong ties between law and information still in effect? They are, but definitively in other forms and formats! One of the major reasons for this newly conceived situation is the modern expansion of lingual types. Until approximately the eighties of the last century, there was no plurality in the types of language available. The analog type of language determined the expression of legal ideas, forms and feelings, and also the architecture of the body of law in its entirety as 'legal dogmatics'.

That changed since the days we bought our first laptop. Today our landscape is completely different, as well as the experience of our bodily movements, meanings, and senses. Our hands are holding intelligent apparatus; our eyes are reading texts and images that are incomparable with the texts we studied in our first years at school, our movements changed even when we walk in unknown streets of cities we never visited before. And more than that our knowledge became slowly profiled as limited: scientific experiments showed in how far our traditional thought patterns including logic, deduction, comparison or conversion did not relate with what experiments about atomic and subatomic particles and their patterns of movement teach us today in technologies that were unimaginable in earlier decades. How are the ties of all of this with the law and legal discourse?

The question seems ridiculous, and often socially irrelevant. Transposed in analog language are conversions between different types of languages indeed illustrating the traditional patterns of the relevance of law in society, or do they also change this view? In other words the book offers questions expressed in analog language about the changes of language type through rethinking. But this Brief is unique in referring to language conversions, which determine law and its social functioning: conversions within the domain of *analog* language, of *digital* language and of quats in *quantum* technologies. They are an ultimate and exemplary activity of a conversion process that is "as such" and "as being itself" continuously in conversion. Those types of information occupy our minds and determine modern research in social, as well as in natural sciences. This is the fundamental challenge the Brief offers the lawyer or any social worker, which may lead to an emphatic viewpoint amidst all inconsiderate changes of positions in human language and expressivity.

Leuven, Belgium
February 2020

Jan M. Broekman
Frank Fleerackers

Contents

Chapter 1
Conversion—A Matter of Principle

Abstract Rethinking legal thinking is entering the stream of thought formations characterized as law in the course of ages. But it requires also an insight in the signs and signals visible at the horizon of the third decade of this century. The latter should receive a name to be recognized in the rethinking process as well as in outlines studying future thought patterns. The name proposed in this Brief includes those signs and signals as well as their horizon and is thus: 'conversion jurisprudence'. Conversion is a simple expression, which became often equalized with 'transference', 'translation' or 'transition', even 'metanoia'; but since the days of the generalization of our digital culture the term received more and more attention in scientific and social media. It is a sign that a rethinking law should not be misunderstood as being an attempt to re-write fragments of the *history* of legal thought formation.

In the eighties of the last century, legal theories and thought patterns of philosophical nature demonstrated a unique pattern of viewpoints and positions that were mostly contrasting. They represented thoughts of positivist, empirical, pragmatic, system-theoretical, natural law, structural, institutional or Critical Legal Studies Movement approaches, which were debated at all levels in Occidental culture as if they were fundamentally different from each other. The scene illustrates that a multitude of opinions characterized legal thought formation for almost half a century.[1] A rethinking reaction tends to formulate how the common denominator at stake was 'opposition to another viewpoint' and the results of this multileveled partitioning always the outcome of a debate pertaining to conflicts. And today?

The thesis of this rethinking process suggests that a new terminology expressing different ideas, attitudes and awareness is indeed at the horizon. *Focus is on a cosmic perspective and a digital culture, which both characterize an actual unfolding that favors a wholeness that encompasses analytics and conversions that absorb partition.* The two form a major nerve of rethinking law and legal thought, and color many dimensions of today's legal experiences. Growing awareness about the cosmic powers influencing terrestrial situations seem to have put the Cartesian *ego* and its boyish *cogito ergo sum* in perspective. An intense activation of the power of conversion has

[1]Ritter and Gründer (Eds.) (1992, 315, 343).

J. M. Broekman and F. Fleerackers, *Legal Thoughts Convert*, SpringerBriefs in Law, https://doi.org/10.1007/978-3-030-43517-2_1

diminished the fashionable identity issue of getting 'lost in translation'. The newly arising notions of wholeness and conversion already heavily influence life-prospects in the third decade of this century. They are almost impossible to fixate scientifically or philosophically and color all components of the concept because their character of *change*. Some explications serve therefore as a first, often provisory, grip to actively participate the rethinking ahead.

Many law journals and publications on legal theory were vividly engaged in debates, which constituted Legal Theory as well as a Philosophy of Law. Even 'holism' was (if mentioned at all) representing a position opposed to 'relativism'. Were these indeed: 'positions', and if so, what was their content, meaning and sense? The question arises whilst rethinking that period of legal thought formation. In retrospect, we experience that the pure existence of those multiple theories and thought patterns challenges our rethinking to decide in how far this *partitioning* is overcome today and whether other foundational views are at stake in our contemporary society's law and legal thought patterns. Such a general process touches the foundations of knowledge and life's attitude but also the specificities of the discipline rethought.

Both are captured as *processes in change*. As was formulated, we refer in that context to the concept of '*wholeness*' and the concept of '*conversion*'. The two are closely affined but by no means identical. The first dominates a general process of knowledge as linked to the foundations of Occidental culture; the second represents genetic processes in a more technical sense linked to specific disciplines. But, beyond doubt: both reinforce each other and share attitude and structures of development inherent to our rethinking activity. And, what should mark this introduction: wholeness and/or conversion are absolutely not unknown as important viewpoints to consider in the debates of the last century. But they were always tied to partitions and partitioning discourses. Never were they a point of unfolding or a position *before* any differentiation takes place and thus *before* an appeal to wholeness unfolds.

Conversion was a seldom-mentioned process in those thought patterns; it was mainly understood from technical points of view and never related to any in-depth ontological statements. Our rethinking will therefore not introduce those two notions as new concepts to consider, but as well-known ideas to revaluate. This requires an important connotation. Conversion has often, also in today's actuality, been understood as 'ethical turn' because it has been understood in proximity to *metanoia* and therefore as a switchover from *logos* to *ethos*. The argument is, that this switch will take the form of religious prophecies as well as revolutionary rhetoric or works and viewpoints of philosophical or literary nature.[2] But our understanding of the components of the term 'conversion' has changed and does no longer cover the switch as mentioned. In conversions intertwined with analog as well as digital types of language (their cultural backgrounds included) one encounters (a) a predominant change of authority (which plays an important role in law and legal discourse), and (b) of means of expression (which indicates the importance of language in the context of understanding conversion) as well as (c) of the Speaker–Hearer Model that masters our utterances at all levels, the linguistic levels included.

[2] Avanessian and Hennig (2019[2], 180).

Those thought patterns present a more general difficulty when we relate *conversion* and *rethinking*. A surprising number of questions arise in that case. Is human thinking more than just an object of conversion? Or is that thinking to be put in perspective, because it results only from the illusory pretence of man being the Crown of Creation? In other words: can our thinking and re-thinking ever become a converting force at the level of conversion? We should after all take into account, that all conversions are already in themselves a continuous process of converting. Our thoughts might participate in that never-ending process—but are they really constitutive forces in that context, or just a direct object? There is no conversion without the power of human imagination, we agree. But do we have the philosophical impetus to distinguish thinking and imagining? Are we able to bridge the gap between the two? Are we able to re-think the gap at all? That would include a possibility to determine and master specific points of our knowledge resulting from our thoughts. But when we create a grip on conversion as a means of acquiring knowledge about reality, on what do we focus our power? If we would know the profile of that power, we would also be able to grasp conversion as a process that is open to human knowledge. But *thinking conversion* is not a form of instrumental thought formation. More precisely formulated: can we, who are used to process partition in order to know, sustain any of our trusted forms of thinking when conversion is at stake? Any answer to this question is debatable. Thinking conversion seems a matter of participation rather than guiding or steering. There is no 'self' that acts as the originators of thoughts and thought products, there is no road ahead of the thinker and there is no profiled field of problems to solve or goals to achieve. There is, to use a metaphoric expression, a *cloud* that makes us experience the multidimensionality of thoughts and thinking —no Speaker-Hearer model. In that regard is "rethinking conversion" a contradiction in itself: conversion energy is the energy to rethink in new lights. It means: not only the "re-", the object of thought, but also and at an equal level is the "think-", the process itself, differing from individualisms and related conventional patterns. We thus already formulated an act of rethinking as "entering the stream of thought formations".

Note in this context, that in particular our partitioning power dominated daily life as well as our philosophical attitudes until today. They unfolded from every thinkable viewpoint. It seemed *our* power, *our* specifically *human* power that leads to answering whatever question comes up or whatever challenge we are confronted with.[3] It means in essence, that our rethinking is fundamentally endangered: its tradition places analysis on the basis of a most general and ontologically relevant process of partitioning *before* any judgment. That becomes clear if we consider our thought patterning, and become aware how we substantiate when we think, and do not consider in what sense our thinking is merely a *form* of our existential human thought formation. We lost awareness of it because of the wealth of possibilities for articulating our ideas: we divide, separate, compartmentalize, explain, oppose, differentiate, split, cut, slice, disjoint and alienate and do not stop to call such

[3]Broekman (2016, 203 ff).

articulations 'language' or in other cases: 'communication'. Will that approach unveil the mysteries of a human existence? Is the emphasis on language correct?

Chomsky answers the question indirectly. He formulates in his 2016 publication: "if we are biological organisms, not angels … much of what we seek to understand might lie beyond our cognitive limits—maybe a true understanding of anything, as Galilei concluded, and Newton in a certain sense demonstrated." He formulates in the same context a truly supportive notion, which should remain a motive in our rethinking process. "That cognitive reach has limits is not only a truism but also a fortunate one: if there were no limits to human intelligence, it would lack internal structure and would therefore have no scope: we would achieve nothing by inquiry."

It is as if Chomsky issues a serious warning to all who have unlimited expectations of a developing *Artificial Intelligence*! Boundaries of human cognition are in this light a true challenge to keep modesty in order not to expand human intelligence into nothingness. In as far as our knowledge in the realm of natural sciences is concerned, Chomsky refers while *discussing wholeness by means of referring to conversion*. We thus read: "We might think of the natural sciences as a kind of *chance convergence* (OUR ITALICS) between our cognitive capacities and what is more or less true of the natural world. There is no reason to believe that humans can solve every problem they pose or even that they can formulate the rights questions; they may simply lack the conceptual tools, just as rats cannot deal with a prime number maze.[4]"

A challenging view indeed: will our rethinking law be able to acknowledge that lawyers 'can solve every problem they pose or even that they can formulate the right questions'? We will experience, that the safety measures law has taken are in the institutionalizing of its discourse and its ensemble of social activities. Is this self-inducing measure apt to meet conditions of human knowledge as such?

Wholeness surpasses each partition.

The tree is seen before I see its leaves. Its branches are perceived as many times as I met the tree as tree: leaves can show me their difficulties too survive, their lack of water or light, their damages caused by insects or birds. But the tree is there. He or she fascinates me, has my attention in a different manner from its leaves or colors, position in the wood or garden. I feel the tree like I feel my life as a unity before my compassion with the damaged leaves unfolds.

The crime is there before I see its dimensions. Its causes and effects seem to be separated from the essentials of the crime: not the harm to people, the disturbed lives of individuals, the wounds of the souls of participants are the main issue—no, the crime as a whole fascinates and disturbs. The lawyer as well as the judge has to determine components, causes, consequences, perhaps social considerations but for me who rethinks the legal context of the crime, the history of our feelings and the actuality of my shocking is dominant: there I am, not in the pattern of a lawyer's causalities.

Rethinking her literary lines and thoughts, the American poetess Susan Howe describes how she wanted "to transplant words onto paper with soil sticking to their roots—to go to meet a narrative's fate by *immediate access to its concrete*

---

[4]Chomsky (2016, 104 f).

totality (ITALICS ARE OURS) of singular injections, crucified spellings, abbreviations, irrational apprehensions, collective identities, palavers, kicks, cordials, comforts." She thus adds: "I wanted jerky and tedious details to oratorically bloom and bear frit as if they had been set at liberty or ransomed by angels."[5]

As a result, she annotates:

Perception crumbles under character
Present past of imminent future

Indeed, we learn that insight into wholeness has its consequences for experiencing time. The future is already there: in wholeness—long before we can notify differences between past and present.

The contract is there before I see its components. Its presence puts my life in perspective. How much power and human or inhuman participation is at stake? The desire of communication and reliable contact overwhelms. What shares have its legal components? What profile has my participation: that of humaneness or of blind desire to possess—my history and the developments of my own culture do enforce me to pose the question: does the contract fit to my soul, and does the law assist me? Can I withdraw from partitioning and see the contract before its single leaves or fruits are visible? Will that experience be legally valid? Or is the gap between tree and contract indicating the artificiality of legal thought formation?

References

Avanessian, M., & Hennig, A. (2019[2]) *Metanoia. A speculative ontology of language, thinking, and the brain*. London: Bloomsbury Academic.
Broekman, J. M. (2016). *Meaning, narrativity, and the real*. Switzerland: Springer.
Chomsky, N. (2016). *What kind of creatures are we?*. New York: Columbia, UP.
Howe, S. (2015). *The quarry, new directions Paperbook original.*
Ritter, J., & Gründer, K. (Eds.). (1992). *Historisches wörterbuch der philosophie, Band 8, lemma's rechtsphilosophie, and rechtstheorie* (pp. 315 ff, and 343 ff). Basel: Schwabe & Co. https://www.schwabeonline.ch/schwabe-xaveropp/elibrary.

[5]Howe (2015, 53).

Chapter 2
Legal Thinking

Abstract Indeed, a flow of information is like the life-ensuring breath we take in the woods, at the seashore or in the centre of our town. Those experiences vary with their surroundings and in particular with the other people creating spaces and thoughts. The jurist's situation is not different, as this Brief suggests, and a first chapter on legal thinking unfolds. Continuity is the main feature of conversion; conversion the climate of re-thinking law. Attention pertains to the person who originates thoughts and ideas, and in his or her ingenuity needs other persons and institutions, norms and values as well as the drive to share what comes to the fore. Legal thoughts are thus unfolding and in this activity they convert. They do not simply add to what is there: their adding is not only a sharing but always also a conversion. Upcoming thoughts in law are not solely the result of what law students or judges, politicians or legal scholars have in mind: they do mainly stem from social experiences and existing thought patterns that are converted already in to law. Legal thoughts demonstrate simultaneousness and even entanglements rather than ordered chains of concepts and ideas. This is mirrored in the first chapter of this Brief—the multiple consequences of the gap between rule and reality with which the jurist is confronted. They determine his or her social position as well as the variety of theoretical viewpoints, so that interaction among them is needed and affectivity a requirement to bring converting legal thoughts to the fore.

2.1 Law, Lawyer and Judicial Thoughts

Can one reduce legal thinking to mere juridical or normative thought? Such conclusion may derived from the categorical way of thinking, broadly used in legal reasoning: a form of fixated and fixating thought, grounded in an understandable but mostly fallible quest for (legal) certainty. This thinking of what is understood as 'law' mirrors the certainty that truth, reality, even law and justice, are to be 'found' through instruments taught in Law Schools and administered in legal practice. But the insight that legal thinking proceeds in- and through interactivity requires a leap of thought. Until today, magistrates experience little impetus in their professional interactivity and common interaction that influence their adjudicative processes caused

J. M. Broekman and F. Fleerackers, *Legal Thoughts Convert*, SpringerBriefs in Law, https://doi.org/10.1007/978-3-030-43517-2_2

by changes in society and patterns. Perhaps a collegial decision that causes any interaction may be found in the shadows of a courthouse. Yet diverse forms of deliberative consultation allow magistrates to ascertain their own prejudices and open their thoughts in favour of change and transformation. That is the conversion they witness when they analyze a 'case': the myriad determining factors (or 'affectors') as such never reduced or reducible to categorically identified elements of 'law'. This Brief aims to point out the importance of such a conversion for practicing jurists and anyone focusing on 'reading law'.

2.1.1 Case and Law

Don't forget: laws are rules and rules embrace, in every aspect, norms. They crystallize principal values and patterns of behaviour. Rules often conflict, but their application is formalized in a case. Law as such is non-existent without precedents and cases as its juridical realization. Law is realized in and through cases—even though 'realization' may sound awkward in context. Actual legal thinking is not merely formalized in a case but encompasses the case in its uniqueness. Thinking the law in and through cases is as differential and dynamic as the case itself. Evidently, such a type of thinking requires an approach that differs from a generic understanding of human through processes. Any such approach will adapt to an ongoing reality. In each case, reality shows itself to the jurist, because values and norms are realized in- and through cases. Not a single case adheres to existing legislation: each case is factually new, different and essentially variable. A judge's thinking is a thought *process* that bridges the divide between rules and cases. This bridging will always depart from the case, not the rule. As such, one should refrain from simply categorizing European continental law as *codified* and Anglo-Saxon law as *casuistic*. Both legal systems thrive on legalism and application thinking, no matter whether this application involves statutes or precedents.

Law finds its realization only in cases. The latter leave legislation to be implemented by the judge. This influences the dynamics of conversion, which determines the generation of meaning. Still, the act of speaking (and language in general) remains essential in legal thinking. Law is speaking from the case: it is a two-way process during which legal norms are verified in casuistry and cases realize law. Dynamics are ideally optimized as long as a judge is not reaching a decision in a case. This also means that judges, when eventually deciding a case, effectuate a shutdown of dynamics. What happens with the case (and its dynamics) when judgment is reached? This is an important aspect of conversion, as it continues the dynamics of legal practice. Even opting for any specific legal procedure invokes qualification and categorization. The latter are fed by a jurist's thinking in general rather than by his or her understanding of the case at hand. Procedural justice does for that reason not lead to effective justice, because no single procedure is intrinsically neutral. Any such suggestion will indeed reflect a particular policy.

The fundamental position of casuistry in law is a consequence of the human quest for certainty and the need for predictability, i.e.: similar cases will be decided similarly, whoever the judge may be. O.W. Holmes Jr's warning fiercely resonates here: "Who constitutes the law? You will find some text writers telling you that it is something different from what is decided by the courts …, that it is a system of reason, that it is a deduction of principles or ethics or admitted axioms or what not, which may or may not coincide with the decisions. But if we take the view of our friend the bad man, we shall find that he does not care two straws for the axioms or deductions, but that he does want to know what the … courts are likely to do in fact. I am much of this mind. The prophecies of what the courts will do in fact, and nothing more pretentious, are what I mean by the law."[1]

2.1.2 Legal Argumentation

No classic research on legal argumentation may therefore suffice to understand the casuistic dynamics of performing judgments in law. The way a judging magistrate thinks becomes only visible in his actions, that is: when he is prepared to bare his thought process via and as interaction. Even though the judge may limit himself at first to a static apprehension of presented determining factors, social interactivity will allow him to find the case's underlying dynamic affectors. When confronting the latter with his prima facie reading of the case, he will be able to map possible solutions against a hierarchy of "affective factors".

One should not lose sight of the dynamic forces active in his thoughts and actions through the conversion of meaning. Affective legal thinking provides a clarifying view of these forces, notwithstanding a judge's personal leanings or juridical intuition. Experienced jurists will offset their own train of thought with the legal affective analysis at hand. This is why interactivity coincides with legal affectors as a case's determining factors, functioning as an instrument to approach the case's changeability as closely a possible.

The term "affect" refers in this context to Gilles Deleuze and Félix Guattari's *Mille Plateaux*. These authors do not limit the concept to personal sentiment or mere emotion. On the contrary, affect is defined, not unlike Spinoza's affectus, as the human capacity of affecting and being affected by one another. Deleuze even posits it as an essential human capacity. Each theoretical and static analysis will remain enclosed in its rationalizing stance, while every case is indeed affective in its essence. As such, cases are witnessed as obstacles to and in any rationalizing analysis, which is evidently not so in its affective alternative.

This affect, understood as a human capacity, is even more essential for law than the purported governing capacity of human reason. The latter is static, while an affective analysis mirrors a case's interactivity and dynamics. Legal thinking thus requires more than a mere juxtaposition of arguments, because the latter may only function

[1]Holmes (1897, 457f.).

as instrumental aids and even cloud the actual affectors. It is therefore not the human capacity of reason, but the capability in- and through interactivity to understand the differential and dynamic aspects of cases as well as their essential changeability. At the same time, jurists will have to see themselves as participating actors with similar affectors (γνῶθι σεαυτόν). The latter will only lead to a clear profile if the inherent dynamics of conversion are exposed. Unveiling the continuing conversion of meanings and their conceptual content as well as language typology (analogue and digital) will enhance such understanding among the legal profession and the public.

2.1.3 Interactivity

Legal procedures are dynamic processes enhanced by interactive practice to optimize an understanding of reality require not only interactive education of jurists, but also a continuing refinement of judicial codes and conduct. Magistrates could develop provisional decisions, requiring parties' response, while facts are being scrutinized and interpreted. But ultimately and evidently, collegial decision-making should prevail. This is not to say that interactive meaning generation would always hold sway in all forms of collegial decision-making. Even collegial processes involving three or more magistrates illustrate many examples of non-interactivity. The same is observable when cases are simply divided among judges or when certain magistrates weigh in too heavily (or too little). But such faults are easily circumvented since codes of procedural conduct will clearly state how collegial decision-making is to be organized. Legal processes are directed by a court president who, not unlike a theatre-director, will instigate their effectiveness. This involves a trespassing on the institutional force of law, which strictly posits speakers and actors into seemingly innocent positions. The same can be said of prosecuting magistrates. Whoever does not function optimally (together) will be replaced, albeit because of functioning badly or too effectively.

Ideally, diversity is a key and interactivity needs to be upheld. If members of a collegial decision-making process think too identical, then their unity and uniformity in qualification would reduce reality to a lethargic substrate. Their effective legal practice would become futile at the expense of vanishing cases. This is how juridical interactivity evolves into a form of encounter, allowing for jurists to somewhat liberate themselves from particular convictions or thought patterns. Interaction provides them with a means to distance themselves and shift their static positions to processes of changeability. At the same time, juridical interaction allows for a juxtaposition of opposing insights, at a distance of fixating rationalization. Only by dynamically exploring and recognizing differing insights, legal thinking will adopt and pervade them, leading to the eventual judgment. Even when concerning truth in a seemingly objective sense, true insight still demands interactive guidance in order to transfer and transmit the meaning of said truth. Juridical interaction prevails when such processes are at stake.

In this context, interaction is understood as crucial in the generation of meaning. Magistrates should accept interaction as the most essential capability for decision-making, which allows them to confront their own case analysis with those surrendered by their colleagues or by parties and their lawyers. A threefold conclusion results here. First, this shows how one's own analysis only divulged a (limited) part of the case, notwithstanding one's conviction to the contrary. Second, this leads to a critical understanding of the way one's analysis is marred by often-unknown prejudices. Third, this points out how one's own analysis unwillingly and often unconsciously resulted in static categorization. Conversely, the interactive confrontation with other magistrates provides for three remedies: enhancement and deepening of one's own analysis; mutual verification of one's prejudices; and an interactive, dynamic understanding of the case's evolving and changing reality. In this sense, interactivity is the central mode of law and legal thinking. The classic Socratic syndrome suggests that mankind is keen on jumping to conclusions and accordingly sticking to its guns, as our thinking presupposes that we, i.e. jurists, have a reasonable capability to understand the world and reality in accordance to categorical and comparable entities.

At the heart of this syndrome resides a dual denial of two core paradigms in human existence, as difference and dynamics constitute essential traits of every real life case, obviously contradicting the inherently static identification of classic legal thinking. Magistrates should therefore adhere to collegial decision-making as a form of mutual confrontation and interactive analysis, encompassing as well as dynamic and differential, optimally approaching a case's reality. Such an interactivity, however, requires individual development of one's own capacity to think, by way of summoning a scale of changeability, generating dynamics from within while appropriately reflecting the specificity of each case and allowing for an authentic, above all effective (legal) decision.

2.2 Formative Social Forces in Law

Social forces at play in the legal world regard adherence to past decisions as well as to stipulated (general) rules. Simply put, two strands of legal structure enclose both forces: precedent based law on one hand, statute law on the other. Their titles already indicate how social interests may play their roles without insurgencies or other forms of revolt.

2.2.1 Precedents and Statutes

It is interesting to see how Anglo-Saxon precedent-based law and European-continental statute law similarly undervalue the importance of day-to-day casuistry. Precedent-based legal systems, as much as their continental counterparts, focus on qualification and categorization techniques that underplay the case's changeability, bearing in mind their fixation on legal certainty. As statute law views cases as objects of legal norms to be applied whereas precedent-based law prioritizes comparative categorization and similitude to divergence. Both types of law do not allow for the differential and dynamic components of legal thinking to flourish. Both types reduce reality to a static substrate of what ever was, or could ever become. Both systems hold limited space for a case's differential and dynamic attributes, or for a case-driven analysis and implementation. This touches the social foundations of law, even though often unnoticed, when they surface as social forces in particular forms of protest, revolt, or anarchism, thus unveiling how such forces even dissemble in theoretical construct and (legal) traditions, as recent schools of thought like legalism, realism, proceduralism, textualism and pragmatism may show.

2.2.2 *Legalism*

Legalism has been accurately defined by Judith Shklar as a form of application thinking, which is not that much limited to the legal realm, but omnipresent among human beings. This apprehension of reality presupposes an understanding or real life as a collection of comparable occurrences. Within a legal framework, such apprehension requires a judge to remain bouche de la loi, where a government of laws, not men established the rule of law. Legislators legislate and judges adjudicate as if the relation between law and society would straightforwardly be one-on-one, and as if reality is at a standstill, petrified. This juridical apprehension contends reality to be inclined towards similarity and regulation, at the same time undervaluing a magistrate's inherent humanity. Assertions of mistrust towards judges and a gouvernement des juges are rationalized by way of compulsive legalism, in order to preclude personal or political excesses. Such distrust often has adverse consequences, whenever judges are (blatantly) politically appointed. Yet there's no effective theory on how to adjudicate when the law remains silent. Theory mostly remains circumscribed to modes of interpretation, where text outranks factual goals and legal certainty remains stuck in a (juridical) quagmire.

2.2.3 *Realism*

Realism originated as a reaction to legal positivism gone legalism, even though the latter allowed for moral independence, i.e. morality loosening its grip on law. If it hadn't been for legalism, procedural law would never have substantiated the way it did. Nevertheless, the inherently artificial confinement gave way to unacceptable excesses in the course of the twentieth century, epitomized by references to "Befehl is Befehl" during the Nuremberg Trials: as long as correct procedure was observed, actions were deemed legal: they were regarded morally reprehensible, yet juridically legal. Evidently, this is narrow legal thinking at its best, and linked to strong foundational references to (internationally) shared values as formulated in the European Convention on Human Rights or the Universal Declaration. Nevertheless, such references resuscitate the topic and influence of morality within and above the legal domain. Consequently one wonders how morality in its manifold forms can be kept at bay, while still upholding an intrinsic morality of law, at least related to its democratic origins. Legal realist scholars like O.W. Holmes Jr., Karl Llewellyn and Jerome Frank showed, early on in the twentieth century, how law and politics are intertwined.[2] Their casuistic and result driven approach, building on philosophical pragmatism by John Dewey, William James and Charles Sanders Peirce, was rejuvenated at the end of that very same century in the Critical Legal Studies Movement of jurists like Roberto Mangabeira Unger and Duncan Kennedy.

2.2.4 Legal Process

The focus on the Legal Process school was a clear reaction to legal realism, even though scholars like Henry Hart and Lon Fuller suggested a middle way between a politically inspired legal realism and the juridical formalism of legal positivism.[3] Their pursuit for neutral, impartial, procedural principles and a specific legal morality failed, as well as a reconciliation among both strands of thought. On one hand, Hart rightly characterized Fullers inner morality of law as a mere deontology.[4] On the other, the legal process school still treated cases as objects of categorical thinking, embedded in categorizing procedures. Finally, the school was viewed as yet another strand of classic legalism, i.e. "thin proceduralism".[5] Nevertheless, criticism of legal realism expanded even further.

2.2.5 Originalism

Textualism or originalism can be seen as the most successful antithesis to legal realism and the *Critical Legal Studies Movement.* As the intersection between law and politics is publicly debated, it is interesting to focus on particular criticism by Alex Kozinski, the then president of the United States Court of Appeals for the Ninth Circuit: "Just to prove that even the silliest idea can be pursued to its illogical conclusion, Legal Realism spawned Critical Legal Studies. … I am here to tell you that this is all horse manure. … judges exercise their powers subject to very significant constraints. … The first, and to my mind the most significant, is internal: the judge's own self-respect. … The second important constraint comes from your colleagues.

---

[2] Holmes (1897), Llewellyn (1930, 1960), Frank (1930).

[3] Fuller (1964).

[4] Hart (1958, 593f.), Fuller (1958, 630f.).

[5] Posner (2008).

If you're a district judge, your decisions are subject to review by three judges of the court of appeals. If you are a circuit judge, you have to persuade at least one other colleague, preferably two, to join your opinion. … (But) what you absolutely cannot get away with is abandoning legal principles in favour of results on a consistent basis. A judge who tries to do this cuts deeply into his credibility…".[6] After rejecting legal realism and the more recent *Critical Legal Studies Movement*, he then forwarded his predilection for textualism or originalism as forms of a reclaimed legalism: "Now, there is an unspoken premise to what I have said, namely that there are more or less objective principles by which the law operates, principles that dictate the reasoning and often the result in most cases. I know you are taught to doubt this in law school, as I was; it is nevertheless true. … one principle I think is extremely important: Language has meaning. … language used in statutes, regulations, contracts and the Constitution place an objective constraint on our conduct. … lawyers complain, with good reason, that within the same circuit there will be two lines of authority on the very same subject. The two lines go off in different directions without acknowledging each other's existence, like ships passing in the night. In such circumstances lawyers have much difficulty in advising clients how to conduct their affairs, the rule of law depending on who the judges in their case happen to be." And yet, it is that very same Kozinski who consequently admits: "We all view reality from our own peculiar perspective, we all have biases, interests, leanings, instincts. … It is important to follow those instincts, because they can lead to a crucial issue that turns out to make a difference. But it is even more important to doubt your own leanings, to be skeptical of your instincts. My prescription is … to fight them. … Is (the) result justified by the law, fairly and honestly applied to the facts? Or is it merely a bit of self-indulgence?" Within the US Supreme Court, the late Antonin Scalia was viewed as a crucial proponent of textualism or constitutional originalism,[7] as he would coin the phrase. Such originalism would lend priority to the actual text or meaning of the Constitution. Still, the same Scalia called himself a faint-hearted originalist and allowed for a certain amount of pragmatism when plain textualism would apparently hinder an effective application of the law. Scholars like Ronald Dworkin would argue for reconciliation, construing law as a specific mode of political morality, yet epitomized by historical, often textual, readings,[8] unless not compatible with a deeper constitutional objective.

2.2.6 Pragmatism

Posner describes judging, as performed by his fellow magistrates, as a form of pragmatism. Beyond his criticism of legalism as well as legal realism, for their fixation on procedure or on political ideology, he portrays a highly personal, experience-based

[6]Kozinski (1993), O'Brien (2012).
[7]Scalia (1984), Tribe (1985, 45).
[8]Dworkin (2011, 413).

view of legal thinking, focusing on the consequences of adjudication: "pragmatic adjudication by judicial concern for consequences … rather than conceptualisms or generalities." In line with philosophical pragmatism, he concentrates on human intuition, or more specifically, on the way magistrates develop a uniquely legal intuition over the years of their profession.[9] While canvassing the classic tension between principle and pragma, between foundation and praxis, he adamantly embraces the pragmatist school, as he joins O.W. Holmes Jr. in rejecting the simplicity of logical deduction in law, as well as John Dewey, in thinking forward instead of backward, positing empiricism above mere deduction.[10] Criticizing principled thinking in a legal context is understandable, whereas the absence of a morally-neutral position underscores the importance of casuistry, and the weighing of principles. But on the other hand, pragmatism holds a risk of slippery slope or stepping stone reasoning, causing principles to gradually wither away.

Posner is the pragmatist who focuses on what effectively works, denouncing formalism and legalism, yet only when their application clearly falters: "(they) cannot resolve tough cases". But he also criticizes legal realism, when "vulgarly political" or "lacking in content".[11] In the heart of his narrative, Posner elaborates on how legal pragmatism may offer solutions at the crossroads of law and morality, of principle and praxis: "what counts as an acceptably pragmatic resolution of a dispute is relative to the prevailing norms of particular societies: pragmatism provides local rather than universal guidance to judicial action".[12] He bases this pragmatism in the context of a legal system where judges "must play by the rules of the judicial game". Even the rigorously procedural thought process of the legal process school, though focusing on impartial and analytical judges, pales in comparison with how legal pragmatism focuses on a case's consequences, thus resulting in yet another articulation of legalism. Proceduralism is the formalist mode of principled thought, where (neutrally) procedural principles endure the same thin and empty treatment as substantive principles. For Posner, proceduralism and legalism are schools of the past, while pragmatism epitomizes present and future.[13] He concludes that: "the good pragmatist judge is not a shortsighted pragmatist. He is not a philosophical pragmatist. But he is a constrained pragmatist": constrained, yet also self-composed, and as such restrained, abiding by the rules at hand: "the pragmatic judge must play by the rules of the judicial game, just like other judges. The rules permit the consideration of certain types of consequences but forbid the consideration of other types. They limit the judge to being … a 'rule pragmatist'".[14]

Interestingly, Scalia's "faint-hearted originalist" and Posner's "constrained pragmatist" seem to find each other in a similar quest for effective law.

---

[9]Posner (2008, 107).

[10]Posner (2008, 232), Holmes (1897, 457), Dewey (1924).

[11]Posner (2008, 238).

[12]Posner (2008, 241).

[13]Posner (2008, 247).

[14]Posner (2008, 254).

According to Posner, judges hide behind application directed thinking: their legalism serves as a pretext to cover up intrinsic constraints, heralding a prototype of legal thought as a merely technical application of rules or norms, even though each and every magistrate is exposed to personal, strategic as well as institutional factors or affectors. Self-knowledge is evidently of the essence.

Posner argues that most judges, even when formally adhering to legalism, de facto succumb to legal pragmatism. In that sense, the need for self-examination is indisputable, not only focused on one's own predispositions, but above all with regard to any and all determining affectors at play: education, background, culture, experience, temperament, identification, preference, ideology, political views, convictions, or even strategic positioning amidst colleagues (e.g. reversal aversion or disproportional respect for higher instances). Hence, he directly links legal or judicial intuition to self-examination (γνῶθι σεαυτόν) as a form of affective analysis. Intuition is in that case defined as a "capability of reaching down into a subconscious respository of knowledge". It is at the same time understood as a form of recognition as well as a plan of action, pointing to experience as a more essential affector (or determining effector) than juridical or procedural reasoning, particularly when the law is "open". In this sense, classic legal reasoning or procedural arguments are mostly ex-post rationalizations as well as justifications of said intuition.

Evidently, human interpretation as a capability is rooted in that very same intuition: "interpretation is an innate, universal and quintessentially human faculty." As such, Posner considers intuition to be more effective than technical analysis.

2.3 Law, Case and Concept

Let us return to the foundational question, which determines not only the behaviour of jurists and citizens, but also the social processes in which their lives unfold. How is legal thinking to be conceived? As if caught amidst a broader identity crisis, coinciding with a heightened sense of urgency against the backdrop of terrorism, a number of interesting monographs have been published[15] on the subject.

In essence, analysis evolved from mere legal interpretation and interpretive techniques or legal reasoning. As such, contemporary analysis should necessarily focus on how legal thinking upholds a particular relation between law and reality by converting juridically posited fields of meaning. Insight into this conversion directly relates to a jurist's self-interpretation and his institutional role.

[15] Sunstein (2001), Dworkin (2008, 2011), Posner (2008), Schauer (2009).

2.3.1 Foundational Structures

Rules and results determine the foundational structures of legal thoughts. Yet the same rule may lead to different results at the hand of jurists, since their thinking emanates from a particular perspective. This personal perspective is more consequential for law than the mere existence of competing rules and their contradictory implementation. A total sublimation of man from law would evidently be useless—not because adjudication by artificial intelligence is unfeasible, but because it would be literally inhuman. The crux of judicial judgment is directed towards human action in all its aspects. Jurists (and judges foremost) will accordingly and ex officio prioritize cases over norms.[16]

Schauer offers a familiar comparison, where a younger child argues to have a 'right' to do something his older sibling was allowed to do at a similar age. He describes forms of reasoning his parents may use, and adds: "For however much these various forms of reasoning do exist throughout our decision-making lives, it is important not to forget that they are odd, and odd in a special way. And this special oddness is that every one of the dominant characteristics of legal reasoning and legal argument can be seen as a route toward reaching a decision other than the best all-things-considered decision for the matter at hand."[17] He thus describes legal thinking as counterintuitive in its focus on cases, and indeed, as both analogy and authority exude a certain institutional effect, they curb as well as restrain a self-evident implementation of doing the right thing.

2.3.2 Case Driven

Jurists are institutionally trained to forgo their initial impulse to instantly opt for a best case-driven solution and abide by generalizing as well as formalist rules (of authority), since human beings, hence also jurists, evidently embrace different opinions with regard to what may constitute a best solution. In other words, such solutions do not automatically, or naturally, follow from the case at hand, yet different people almost automatically, or naturally, adhere to different perspectives on what might be best in casu. To surpass this seemingly irreducible conundrum, which involves rule*s* of men, one may comprehend how the rule of law surfaced as a workable alternative in order to achieve legal certainty in a world confounded with particularisms. Accordingly, as cases incorporate antinomy, they will yield in front of decisions based on rules, analogy or authority. Such definition of judicial thought is understandable and even somewhat defendable. Yet this evidently categorical cure is worse than the disease, as even Schauer concedes. On one hand, we prefer to restrict the obvious perils of fallacious adjudication with an absolute Rule of Law. On the other hand, we

[16] Fleerackers (2000, 52–55).

[17] Schauer (2009, 7).

would like to bolster good and wise decisions by providing for necessary space and headroom, though this would expose the Rule of Law to imperfection and fallibility.

So where does this leave us? Is it 'case against rule', 'man against institution', 'reality against law'?

2.3.3 Case by Case

This is where Cass Sunstein's adage comes in: one case at a time. Yet for Sunstein, prioritization of cases in law is even more important than the singularity of each and every occurrence, or each and every instance of human action. When judges apparently adjudicate with similar future cases in mind, legal thinking itself is at risk. Indeed, and even more so than legislators, judges wield a very limited view of the way future cases may develop. Such criticism evidently strikes at the heart of precedent-based law. Yet the same danger resides in the heart of any adjudication, as courts and tribunals aren't organized and structured to produce such juridically proactive decisions. Caution is indeed advised. Meanwhile, the cautionary essence of one case at a time is certainly at play in effective legal thinking. Rules have a general as well as formal constellation. Yet, underneath such generality and formality, a ratio legis resides. Understanding the effectivity of law and its thought patterns requires an insight in human actions, in rule-governed as well as adjudicative situations, which are susceptible to cognitive illusions. This does not mean that such situations belong to the domain of psychology. Indeed, psychology, philosophy, sociology, economics, as well as law are scientific domains related to human conduct, of which the legal field is primarily concerned with its normative aspects. Hence, rules and rule following are central themes of legal theory and questions regarding the underlying rationale of a rule are at the forefront of legal scholarship and legal education.

A legal rule's formalist as well as generalizing character is foundational to the Rule of Law, in order to uphold legal certainty, i.e. predictability and uniformity of legal decisions, yet also to curtail the decisive powers of individuals, such as policy makers, legislators and magistrates. With regard to its formality, legal rules boast a necessary textual, verbatim and literal character, upholding its weight amongst its non-juridical siblings, illustrating why the letter of the law often prevails and why a judge is somewhat mockingly characterized as "bouche de la loi". As such, both generalizing and formalist aspects of a legal rule adhere to its essence. Aristotle may have put it most clearly, arguing legislation to be universal, general as well as generalizing, while the nature of any case, and of reality for that matter, should be seen as singular and unique. Legal rules require case-by-case adjustment, not because they are inept or inconclusive, but because of their generalizing character. The notion of aequitas[18] (ἐπιείκεια) or equity would soften its harshest consequences. As Aristotle argues in his Ethica, not the rule is at fault but its generalizing stance is at odds with reality. In fact, two worlds collide, the generalizing world of rules and the innate

[18] Waelkens (2015, 326).

particularity of a reality of occurrences or cases. Hence, these worlds are in need of bridging, which, for Aristotle and Cicero, aequitas would provide. In this Brief, focus resides on who realizes such aequitas: the jurist as man of law, epitomizing man and law in crucial conversion.

References

Dewey, J. (1924). Logical method and law. *Cornell Law Quarterly, 10*(1), USA.

Dworkin, R. (2008). *Justice in robes*. Cambridge, USA: Harvard University Press.

Dworkin, R. (2011). *Justice for Hedgehogs*. Cambridge, USA: Harvard University Press.

Fleerackers, F. (2000). *Affective legal analysis*. Berlin: Duncker & Humblot, BRD.

Frank, J. (1930). *Law and the modern mind*. New York: Brentano, (2009^2) Oxfordshire, UK: Transaction/Routledge.

Fuller, L. (1958). Positivism and fidelity to law—A reply to professor Hart. *Harvard Law Review, 71,* Harvard, USA.

Fuller, L. (1964). *The morality of law* (revised ed. 1965). New Haven, USA: Yale University Press.

Hart, H. L. A. (1958). Positivism and the separation of law and morals. *Harvard Law Review, 71,* Harvard, USA.

Holmes, Jr., O. W. (1897). The path of law. *Harvard Law Review, 10*(8), Harvard, USA.

Kozinski, A. (1993). What I ate for breakfast and other mysteries of judicial decision making. *Loyola of Los Angeles Law Review, 26,* 993, Los Angeles, USA.

Llewellyn, K. (1930). *The bramble bush: On our law and its study*, (2009^2) Oxford, UK: Oxford University Press.

Llewellyn, K. (1960). *The common law tradition: deciding appeals*. Brown, Hachette Book Group, New York, USA: Little.

O'Brien, D. (2012). *Judges on judging: Views from the bench* (4th ed.). London, UK: Sage.

Posner, R. (2008). *How judges think*. Cambridge, USA: Harvard University Press.

Scalia, A. (1984). Originalism: The lesser evil. *Cincinnati Law Review, 57,* 849, USA.

Schauer, F. (2009). *Thinking like a Lawyer*. Cambridge, USA: Harvard University Press.

Sunstein, C. (2001). *One case at a time*. Cambridge, USA: Harvard University Press.

Tribe, L. (1985). *God save this honorable court.* New York, USA: Random House.

Waelkens, L. (2015). *Amne Adverso: Roman legal heritage in European culture*. Leuven University Press.

Chapter 3
Jurisdiction

Abstract What does 'law's diction' mean in legal language, when it's meaning in everyday language is a different one? The promising expression 'diction' does *not* refer to publicly understandable, open-minded and dialogue language, and thus *excludes* direct access and participation of the citizen. 'Jurisdiction' is the official term for the institutional power to make decisions and to proclaim judgments that are legally valid. Law's diction is, in other words, "having a say over…" and not a "come, please speak with me". Law's authority is *the challenge to rethink legal language as law's diction*: authority has its own, powerful and precisely detectable linguistic model. It is called the "Speaker-Hearer Model" in all branches and periods concerning the study of language. In law, speech events are congruent with this model and authority as basic to law and legal practice is almost identical with that model's effect and existence. The official "I have a say…" plays a dominating role in the contrasts between legal–and everyday language. The authoritative structure of speech and text in jurisdiction, the dominance of the first person singular and the references to what has been written as institutionally validated law, necessitate indeed a rethinking of the jurisdiction's language in use. There are at least two ways to clarify this situation: (a) in ordinary language is *accomplishment* (i.e. the fact expressed in the 'to say for…') the most important; and (b) in the view of a legal theory proves this statement (the basis of jurisdiction) the necessity of a 'hierarchy of modal values'. Both are important for a 'to say for…' as a hinge of any legal functioning. One has to take the term 'diction' in the larger concept 'jurisdiction' very serious. Law has been spoken, and those utterances were inscribed by means of carving in rocks and pillars millennia ago until today's datafication based on digital techniques. That history is still providing a form for legal thought formation and confirms its factual character all around the pluralities of legal systems. Without rethinking law in the production of its lingual terms, one is left acting color-blind in social life.

J. M. Broekman and F. Fleerackers, *Legal Thoughts Convert*, SpringerBriefs in Law, https://doi.org/10.1007/978-3-030-43517-2_3

3.1 Rethinking the Multi-layered Legal Language

3.1.1 Legal and Ordinary, i.e. Daily Language

All legal language is multi-layered. It provides legal hermeneutics with an extraordinary task to fulfill in legal philosophy and plays a role in every decision or consideration at each level of legal praxis. Rethinking the language(s) of law would therefore always imply a rethinking of the institutional architecture of law and its specified practices, as well as the particular relation of each of those levels with the expressivity in which lawyers need to be engaged. To mention legal- and daily language as levels to consider suggests a clarity, which exists neither in the language of law nor in legal reality's expressivity. Each of those levels is complex in itself, has its own issues of language maintenance and communication and they are often intertwined in manners invisible for those who walk their path in one of them.

So, how can considering language become a reliable bridge between the reality of law and the facts of everyday life? That bridge and the possibilities to reinforce its relations has been a subject of reflection since long. Jacob Israel de Haan, the Dutch lawyer, poet and politician who held in 1916 the world's first Chair in Legal Semiotics at the Amsterdam University, brought this to the fore and concentrated all relevant ideas in the slogan "Betere Taal is Beter Recht" [Better Language is Better Law].[1] His intention is clear: any legal doctrine combines words, terms and concepts, which are not equivalent. Bad language—thus bad law, because "… a single word has not a meaning in itself, but only in a complete sentence. … it has another meaning each time a word is used. Even for a speaker and a hearer is the meaning different." He continues: "The meaning of a word is the intent, which it should convey, the intention of the user."

Words are indeed the preferred instrument of the legal power at hand. The legal text embodies limits of law and legal discourse—not its 'use' by lawyers and judges. This insight parallels the formula of Maturana and Varela, neurophysiologists and biologists in the 1980s, claiming: "*Everything we do is a structural dance in the choreography of coexistence*."[2] The authors were not aware how accurately they pronounced the basics of law and legal practice. Their words approached the dominating opinion of the Signific Circle in Amsterdam and the Vienna Circle.[3] In that regard exists a strong commonness of foundational opinion among the members of both Circles: a fact still to study and to rethink.

[1]Haan (1916, 14–19; 79).

[2]Maturana and Varela (1988, 248).

[3]Schorske (1981, 208 ff).

3.1.2 Street and Court

Street and the Court represent a major region of the diction of law and legal thought formation in general. They are omnipresent in social tensions, often playing a polar role and representing meanings that are highly influenced by digital types of language and communication. Their multilayered character causes difficulties to perform a clear and profiled rethinking. Both are concepts radiating authority, but always an authority beyond a particular expression or a series of expressions in a text. Their character is a general "saying for…"—in the case of the Court a '*saying for law*' and in the case of the Street a 'saying for *truth*'. Court and Street must be rethought as *rhetorical arguments in the sign pool of life*. "Outstanding Court, outstanding Street."—there is no hierarchy without vocabulary; there is a tradition in effect through naming and citing.[4]

The Ancient Greek *agora* was in that sense perhaps a precursor of the street in modern cities. Ruth Padel describes how any *agora* was a center of assembly and commerce with a theatrical character. This structuring has consequences for language as a means of living—exploring the life of citizen, artist, author, orator or politician: "any audience's self-awareness is an aspect of the way that audience completes its play", she notes. However, "plays are put 'in front of us' ", she remarks, not shunning the differences and commonness of 'in' and 'out'. "But at Athens they were acted *inside*: inside the horseshoe circle that embodied the community. The audience's identity as a *self-conscious* member of that community was part of its experience of tragedy. An actor's entry into that space was entry into the attention of those who experienced themselves to be the city. And being the city meant judging, or inferring, the interior of others on the basis of what they had done and said; from how they had, publicly, seemed. The assembly and the law courts were a kind of theater, the theater as an assembly-place, a court. In all these, it was crucial that you could not see inside another person and yet, somehow, you must. You, and the community, must proceed as if you could".[5]

It is also important to underline that the Dionysian and other Festivals, the Tragedies, Dramas and Comedies, were moments of *public order*. Archeological city maps, especially those of Athens in the 5th century BC, show how locations to perform the Festivals were rather accidental and often the socially best place in a changing and expanding city.[6] The choice of location is a strong additional argument to emphasize the specificity of a public order in contrast to any religious, ritualistic or spiritualistic order. The central position of *order* is underlined by the observation that the performance of a Tragedy as fragment of a Festival is a moment of possible

[4]Schorske (1981, 24), describes how around 1860 the *Ringstraße* in Vienna became a visual expression of values and power of a social class, which was a matter of values projected in space and stone, a place of public services, a defense against a flooding Danube river and the development of a public health system.

[5]Padel (1990, 337–339), (1992), Broekman (2017, 1–37).

[6]Calvino (1974, 1997, 65 ff).

public *dis*order. Public order and social disorder were also in those days experienced as signs of a legal system.

In the second, revised edition of the famous *The Dramatic Festivals of Athens* by Sir A. Pickard-Cambridge is explicitly mentioned that Festivals were framed by legally tuned recuperation-sessions, named a *Pro-Agon* to begin and an *Ecclesia* at the end. There were laws applied, which forbad proceedings against debtors during certain Festivals; there was nearly always an Assembly who scrutinized the conduct of officials; there were complaints heard by individuals regarding misconduct or injuries that took place during the Festival. The strong ties between individual life, the public Festival and the court-like sessions held afterwards, were strictly ruled fragments of culture, which mirrored the general image of man in public life. Contests controlled by judges played a central role. Names of participants and procedures with selection were highly influenced by opinions from the public. Judges with the task to focus on the performances of tragedies and comedies differed for instance from those controlling the execution of choruses. Court and Street were seldom so visibly linked together, Pickard researched.[7] Closures of the Festival were concretized not only by public functionaries but also by hundreds lawyers or/and assistant-lawyers—a publicly accepted phenomenon. A sharp contrast between court and street, that is: between legal- and lay language did *not* belong to the experiences of life in Ancient Greece.

The Court-Street relation is truly an old theme in Occidental culture. Legal theory has hitherto hardly taken notice of this event, despite the fact that it that characterizes law's expressivity. The gap between the two lead to the frontispiece of Hobbes' famous *Leviathan* and actual street protests organized and guided by social media illustrate its importance today. The contrast between Court and Street is a noteworthy cultural phenomenon that features the realization of modern citizenship. *Today, the gap should be seen as a landscape and the contrasts solved through focusing on totality.* The gap must in modern eyes become a valley, the landscape a moment of the totality of terrestrial life, its social values and multiple languages, which are held for equal, included.

3.1.3 Legal Language as an Artifice

Rethinking law's language is a complex activity. The latter does not only result from the distance between Court and Street or Judges taking the floor and the Defense articulating. There is a deeper and almost global issue at stake: legal language unfolds in a natural-, but becomes during that unfolding an in essence artificial language. That is what juris*diction* characterizes. Legal diction sounds different from what it means. Its complexity is in the presence of natural language while its components represent

---

[7] Pickard-Cambridge (1991^3, 57 ff). Legal information is in the entire Chapter II: *The City Dionysia*. Emphasis is indeed on the City in contrast to the Rural Festivals, dealt with Chapter I: *The Lesser Festivals*, §c: *The Rural Dionysia*, p. 42 ff.

non-natural meanings. Sounds, meanings and senses of words in natural language are conversed into legal language. That omnipresent *conversion* makes us recourse to the catchword *architecture*. It is like windows, doors, walls, stones, wirings and tubes being equal but in their combination creating very special streets and attractive townships! Natural language words sound in Court like on the street, but they are different because of their different (social) context. The difference is the result of the legal specialist's grip. He selects and reforms meanings of natural words into his legal architecture often named argumentation or even logic. The jurist is an agent mastering meaning, one concludes. A Law School Program illustrates the artificiality of law's language in its structuring of education. Indeed: rethinking law's diction is complex.

The basis of understanding the commonness of *being together in a legally forged situation* is- or is not presented in law's diction: *the artificiality of legal language is the product of a multilevel process of meaning in a society and its cultural foundations.* In other words: it is not the legal thinker resp. the jurist who is responsible for the artificial character of his professional language, but rather the cultural situation in which he or she unfolds specific knowledge and skills. A fundamental change in Occidental culture should be observed: *meanings are not decisive anymore, but types of expressivity*—which create meanings and put them into perspective at the same time. This change from *meaning* to *type* implies an actual change of epistemology. Knowledge is *the product of understanding role and specificity of participation of both subject and object in ultimately cosmic processes*—that is an important message to the Lawyer and his Client, the judge and his Court, the Defense and its socio-juridical context.

A one-sided understanding of "the social" dominates our contemporary social and political philosophy, in particular the idea that 'the social' always relates to a form of 'belonging'. *But the 'street' does not embrace this one-sidedness.* Are social relations thus possible without any defined belonging? The answer is: yes, it is—and that is exactly the case where the desire of the pedestrian is to characterize as *the desire to be a sign alone*—a desire that blind-sighted *Walter Benjamin* in his famous 1927–1940 'Passages'. On the 'street', the walking citizen is socialized even when he or she is not belonging. The rapper, the walker and the smart phone with its tiny screen replacing the many mirrors of the Arcades illustrate how you are with no identity beyond a phone number, an e-mail address or a hash tag. The phantasm of identity reflects only vaguely in the *Selfie* on the street: a more-than-romantic IT issue! Always and everywhere being contactable is the street's phantasm on communication, thanks to its displacement into the virtual world. In other words, the pedestrian can interpret herself as a liberated *Self* only because sociability reaches *beyond* belonging. This observation challenges the hidden romanticism in philosophical positions from *W. Benjamin* to the recent *Invisible Committee.*

It opens hitherto seldom-accessed dimensions of the Self. The spirit of semiotics invigorates the question: when, and under what circumstances, is a meaning a sign? And: when does a meaning lead us to a sign that is 'a sign on its own', as Peirce characterized; when does a sign not have an owner anymore, but becomes recognized as an encompassing issue in its own right? The formula 'the Self as a Sign on its Own' is an almost poetic, post-Kantian as well as post-Peircean positioning of components of the Self, which does *not* place any sovereignty in an *exteriority* of that Self. But Who or What is a Self that restricts itself to an "I say for…" and how does it in that case relate to any exteriority?

We ask: if the qualification 'artificiality' holds, what meaning has it today? Cyber law does not answer such questions, and law's efforts to cope with the particularities of digital language fail in this regard. Several observations belong to the context of that question.

(a) First, the term "artificiality" in the case of a professional language is a matter of analog language and not of any other type or conversion process. What does that mean? Do conversions not transcend the barriers between analog and digital thought patterns?
(b) Second, arguments about the artificial character of what a lawyer articulates, a judge opinions or hermeneutics brings to the fore, lost much of their conviction.
(c) Third, we thus discover that 'artificiality' is rather a *social* commentary than a *linguistic* feature of a legal word. The term fits into a thought pattern constituted by attitudes embracing contrasts and antitheses but not in a view that focuses on all substantial elements as fragments of a specific wholeness named 'law'.

That attitude is the product of a special education. Signs, symbols, meanings and doctrinal forms are important elements in that education process, although they function nearly unnoticed in legal exposés. Students are taught to understand and to practice that language through their study of jurisprudence, judgments, precedents and cases, legal history and related issues, which altogether function as crucial signs in society formatting law's specific conceptual architecture. To study law means often: to study how to manage all relevant references that function as building blocs of the entire discourse. Students are required to master legal writing, legal argumentation, understand the predominant legal hierarchy—who cares, who knows, or who even understands this as long as all those legal instruments function well in the actuality of law's modus operandi?

We mention six catchwords at random. They might outline the modus as follows:

(a) Jurists *create meaning*. Their understanding of law as a system of meanings (often represented by signs) should prevail in all dimensions of legal practice. Existing meanings are conversed into specifically legal meanings, which are often formulated in terms of a natural language. Understanding and mastering that technique brings verbal- and non-verbal communication closer together;
(b) Jurists work on *interpretation*. All arguments and theoretical efforts include the appropriate understanding of interpreting a sign, since "everything there is" can be a sign;
(c) A jurist's activity is always *in process*—this characterization is valid for all dimensions and all occurrences that bear the name "law". All legal knowledge conditions are moments of a flux of events: in this regard does legal discourse not differ from discourses in natural languages;

(d) Jurists work with texts, speech acts, and other articulations; they direct their mastering abilities towards *surface- and deep articulations* (or *phenotext and genotext*). The latter are names for different discourses when articulating reality; they focus on the connectivity between sign and interpretation;
(e) Jurists are aware of the *continuous function of discourses,* which determine the major forms of life in a society via existing legal practices. They select within those forms what is allowed to be a surface of speech or text—hence the term 'architecture in this context. The rich gamma of traditions and habits that supports their mastering is anchored in this discourse;
(f) Jurists always bear the burden of a profiled awareness about *the legal approach to identity*. They keep in mind that linguistic dimensions determine the process of identity formation: an identity unfolds rather through *being spoken to* by others then by *being compelled to speak*.
(g) Jurists are continuously confronted with "*the otherness of the other/Other*"; the expression's multidimensional meaning is not solely describing social communication or other types of understanding/sensibility, for instance where "perceived difference plus recognized otherness" are basic for the sign concept. The legal meaning of otherness (for instance in crime or contract) is by no means identical to what the expression means in a natural language.

But steps in legal work are primarily steps in a milieu of texts. A legal *modus operandi* needs for that reason the *procedures of identification* when constructing a legal text that prepare for a legal judgment. They are:

(1) Identify the *message*. Find and describe the central message in the text by means of concise language and highlight the main issue. Try to already construct a parallel series of remarks pertaining to that message (a) in terms of everyday language and (b) in terms you would use as competing legal expressions;
(2) Identify the *signifiers*. Formulate what they do in this text context and determine their meaning(s). Be aware that a network of signifiers can be detected in natural language and a network of legal signifiers;
(3) Identify the *signifieds*. These are the receptor of meaning conveyed to the reader. Try also to understand what the receptor perceives as the meaning at hand, and determine whether that is identical, equivalent or different from the meaning(s) in legal expressiveness;
(4) Identify the *paradigms* at hand, such as pairs, oppositions, or categories, including their psychological or sociological signification. Have an eye for the language used, whether it is a natural language, a legal language or any mixture or perhaps a suggested translation of the one into the other;
(5) Identify the strings of words or phrases, a collection of statements or propositions that form a specific unity. Find the direct and the indirectly implied messages, which you can identify. Be aware how these syntagmata form clusters in legal discourse, which often times want to be understood as a *sign*. Linguistic components, such as words, de- and connotations, literal and symbolic messages, play altogether a constitutive role because the legal discourse provides coherence in all legal systems;

(6) Identify the *principle* that functions in the text or message such as: "justice" or "peace keeping", "equilibrium", and so on.

Those expressions fulfill a sign-function, and in doing so represent an ideological position, meant to have a strong rhetorical power, as for instance in most master-discourses. It is of rhetorical importance to understand how these textual elements form a distinctive pattern, which refers to the text construction. The latter is a hinge in the multiple conversions, which create the patterns of legal thinking and are thus the basis for legal practice. The artificiality of the language is a most important component of law's practices, which take place in a natural language but is in no way natural! A major consequence is, that an emphasis on the analysis of legal language unveils how probably all positions of legal thinking and practicing constitute 'law' through the application of 'meanings in conversion' and never of one fixated meaning or one complex of semantic components.

Elements of natural language suggest also the possibilities of emotional ties between lawyer and client. But these are not effective without the rational, architectonic dimensions of law's non-natural linguistic components. Note, how emotional dimensions are important in analog language. But there is more to observe. The proudly announced irrelevance of time and space as basic in digital communication is not only a counterpart of these analog actions but also a change and often destruction of human emotions. Modern man's "telling the story" has changed dramatically because the Speaker-Hearer model can no longer be defended as the only position for telling man-and-earth's position. 'Man is no longer the unique Speaker' is a slogan that illustrates sharp changes and bitter occurrences of social nature. Earth, Planet, Cosmos or Globe is no longer simply the Hearer of that Speaker, as millions of scientists around the globe underline today. Is the Twitter-story just a sign of the lacking ability to tell the story? Human selfhood has entered the plurality of language types and their inherent patterns.

3.2 Law's Conversions

Modern law is confronted with social forms in which the *otherness* of others is not appreciated as a *form* of life—which has to be accepted as if it were a natural or God-given phenomenon—but as *a social value* awaiting its actualization by means of law and politics. In other words, a new development includes that meanings of expressions such as "diversity" or "tolerance", "multiplicity" or even "language", relate to a prominent narration, which challenges rather than appeases any social appearance. Moreover, today is a global public confronted with questions how to cope with a large variety of traditions, gender issues, ethnic or religious *differences, which do no longer relate to the concept of 'otherness'* sharing a traditional evidence. That public is, thanks to digital communication as an all-embracing technique, broader than ever before and often a founding social value in life. This seems to provoke special tasks for lawyers and politicians when they have to provide legal support beyond local or regional legal conditions. Politicians tell us that even the most sophisticated types of legal provision do not always satisfy contemporary requirements. This leads to the complaint that modern law does not function the way it should. Law is thus criticized in the context of rethinking legal thoughts.

3.2.1 Conceptual Conversions

This leads to focus on several remarkable conversions, which seem foundational in the unfolding of law as a narrative architecture. We mention *transference*, which is in essence an important conversion in modernity. We further perceive *parallels*, which monitor conversions, and we finally highlight a *profile*, which functions as a system of conversions that does not highlight its exceptional character.

From Diversity to the Plural

First, we take note how *diversity* is treated as *plurality* in many legal, sociological and political publications—no more, no less. The often deep metaphysical problems of diversity as a way to deal with the otherness of others (as in Rosenzweig, Levinas, Peirce, Nietzsche, or Heidegger) became converted into the notion of a *plural* in all its guises. The lives of peoples relate in their plurality character to more specific racial, ethnic, and religious features and minority problems, so that they all should become categorized as plurality in the first place. Uses and techniques of e-communication seem to be consistent with developments from 1948 onwards, when legal instruments were generated after the genocides during the Second World War and the rise of Civil Rights movements.

Rights and Duties

Secondly, we register an often-explored parallel to diversity, which appertains especially to *tolerance*. Philosophers writing about tolerance in the European seventeenth and eighteenth century had a broad understanding of its psychological, religious and political complexity as well as its links with the limits of State power and the law. They were caught up in the adaptability of the human mind, including the good and bad decisions made under the pressure of complex situations. Their focus unfolded mainly on *tolerance* as a *basic value* in modern society. That was an important ethical value, which acquired global dimensions. The conversion at hand is from (1) a mutual pardon to (2) State legal protection and (3) politically enforced respect for fundamental rights and duties.

Image, Profile

The subject of a *third* type of conversion concerns the *image of man in law and legal discourse*. The image as conceived in earlier centuries and mirroring anthropological insights of the time converts into a fixated image of man as the basis for law and legal discourse. It is dominated by the duality of rights and duties—a structure that should be universally valid. Voltaire advocated a mutual pardon, which seems to be the equilibrium of rights and duties that became ascribed in legal terms (possession) to each individual living in different legal and political contexts. The Speaker-Hearer model for language and communication played the role of a general framework.

3.2.2 Language Determination

Language is, and has always been, the riddle of law. Language is law's sole and most reliable instrument and an immeasurable field of search for meaning to be implied in the lives that unfold. But it is in a continuous conceptual struggle with the discourses of everyday-life. Law speaks its own language, anchored in expressions of everyday language without ever being able or allowed to completely identify with it. The distance between the two leads citizens to complain about not understanding how lawyers articulate their problems and strive for justice. Legal language is an artificial language composed of words, expressions and patterns of a natural, everyday language. The effect of the artificial character of language is in the continuous conversion of one in the other, a continuously repeated attempt to master specific meanings and articulations for the goal of maintaining a social order. That attempt characterizes the totality of law's narrative structures and structuring.

Many studies give evidence of a semantic ambiguity that stems from the difference between the languages in which they are embedded. Bayle, Voltaire, Kant and others highlighted tolerance as a feature of the human mind and its social relationships. They were unaware of the fundamental changes in meaning that happen to the concept once it becomes embedded in legal discourse. Many readers naively understand tolerance as an all-embracing social relation, whereas legal research focuses on balancing rights and duties on a global level far from the madding crowd.

This is exactly what Hohfeld encountered when he studied American legal jurisprudence. Balkin stated that a major function of language is to define or fixate what "something is", and that language makes us express ourselves along the lines of those concepts, which we in those uses take for natural. "Just as reality is shaped and created by language, so too legal and political reality is shaped and created by mutually defined legal and political rights, powers, and duties".[8] Hohfeld defined in that perspective a right as a legal guarantee that one has the privilege to engage in certain actions and invoke the power of the State to prevent other persons from engaging in certain other actions. He approaches the borderline between legal and natural language, explaining that a legal interest is always accompanied by a matching interest of at least one *other person*—an interest he calls a "jural-correlative". With that step, he finally finds himself in the domain of specifically legal language.[9]

This insight has consequences for *the position of the reader* of legal texts and texts related to legal discourse. Reading *legal texts* requires entering a specific language discourse. *Texts related to legal texts* (as one meets in novels and other types of

---

[8]Balkin (1990, 1121–1123), Wirth (2011, 157–183).

[9]Hohfeld (1964, 1919, 50).

literature) do *not* require that move! Yet every reader is rooted in a particular language in order to access the world around us and to access others who share our lives. It is thanks to the latter that narrations provide a precious and generally accepted meaning and sense. A reader's thought pattern is anchored in linguistic determinants, which are a common good of the culture in which one lives. The latter engenders surface structures of daily conversations and deep structures that support elementary and most often general significations to unfold. That process of determination through language is, however, by no means a *static* event. *A reader is always a meaningful sign to his or her Self as a result of the act of reading.* That Self is most naturally to the modern jurist: the double-structured language, natural as well as artificial, is a riddle that can never be solved by means of a natural, everyday language. But this double structure of discourse remains a logical necessity when reading legal texts. Any Self is for itself a Sign. Otherness, one concludes, permeates all forms of discourse. The reader encounters that otherness in discourse itself as fluxing opposites, as permeating negations, as fixated grounds, as shadows of truth and falsity.

3.2.3 Narrative- and Conversion Techniques

One should distinguish three legal techniques of conversion: (1) a conversion type with *legal casuistry* as its main determinant, (2) a conversion type with *legal linguistic forms* as its determinant, and (3) a conversion type of *legal semiotic* nature.

(a) *A conversion analysis of casuistry* is for instance a story of racial integration, whereby "integration" is a name for "diversity" on one hand, and "equal protection via integrated school systems", a name for "tolerance", on the other.[10] A narrative approach intertwines fact patterns of the case (race and class), which often show distorted patterns of social knowledge and tenacious prejudices. Law's desire to perform as a master discourse amidst other discourses is one of the major issues in a case-directed legal narrative. It explains as well as certifies qualities of social knowledge deeply embedded in law, legal procedure and discourse.
(b) *Language-directed studies* deal with more abstract and even legal-theoretical issues. Changing language patterns in narrations between groups who directed themselves to the US Supreme Court in the second half of the twentieth century are an example. They mirrored changing socio-economic positions of politically and culturally significant groups. The significance of languages, making use of legal discourse, put civil liberty at the forefront. Civil liberty is a form of understanding constitutional features as a *mark of life in law*".[11]

---

[10]Pencak (2009, 167).

[11]Lewis (2009, 11f).

(c) *Legal semiotic* conversions highlight that *any mutual conversionary grip on meanings is a deep communicative issue* in its own right—legally and philosophically. Peirce remarked that 'two' seem necessary: two partners in communication, from which one is an interpretant and the other the determination of an interpretant by a sign of an object. Conversion aims at both without defining that there are really two. They operate in a single act of understanding to the extent that the act could be characterized as cooperative. Our understanding of cooperation reflects in that case a *schism of the two*.

Narrative- and conversion techniques often seem identical, although they are characterized by different social dynamics. A simple act of reading will provoke a clear tension: how can one *read* a *view*point? What does that mean? And if it means something, is that meaning not manipulated? And, as was said above, if one reads, one reads always an *order,* which is not readable but the result of management in a good or bad sense of the word. How can we draw the conclusion that signs have no intrinsic meaning without considering how signs emerge, Peirce asked whilst pointing out that signs are never simply the product of a dual relation between signifier and signified. The same legal term, which seems to function as a sign, may have different meanings in different jurisdictions, in different fields of law, or even in the same legal code. This offers an insight about knowledge-at-work in legal discourse as explored on a global scale. China, a pluralist legal system embracing traditional law, civil law and common law on an equal footing, explores various jurisdictions. This pluralism can also be understood as an ensemble of *mixed* legal systems—dominant on the globe today. But in communities, which share the same language, the same sign may have different denotations because of the differences of legal systems. Co-existing legal terms which function as a *chain of signifiers* are brought into existence, but the conversions that support this plurality of terms remain in the dark.

A study of the world map of legal systems and signifiers may lead to a deeper understanding of sociological, political and cultural issues that show the *limitation, specificity* and *contextual character* of the study of global law, as well as the necessity to consider the *multicultural* dimension of each legal system, particularly in its practices of reference. Such a map, designed by the Ottawa Law School and its Civil Law Department, provides information about the world geography of legal systems. A true mapping of relevant clue-conversions should be undertaken with this map in hand. There is an important lesson to learn from the world map of legal systems. Civil and Common Law techniques, approaches, and traditions are used for a variety of lifestyles and patterns of culture in the United States, European Union, African, and Asian countries. *The mixing of legal systems seems a more important issue for legal studies than their mutual comparison*. These mixings appeal in a hitherto unrecognized manner to an understanding of chains of legal conversions. Mixed legal systems and forms of life are at the threshold of globalization, and students of law as well as legal scholars must adapt to new trends in law studies and practices with this reorientation in mind. Is *diversity* in the heart of legal discourse a companion of the *plural* features of *mixed* legal systems? The question challenges a theory of conversion in law.

3.3 Discourses Format, Conversions Energize

The *life of a narration has a longer duration than that of a chain of conversions*, the above pages suggested. A discourse makes a something function in a wider lingual context whereas a conversion makes the same matter function in other contexts than a former. Time counts everywhere and in every context. That thought forms a central component of the rethinking endeavor and is axial for our understanding of law as 'conversion jurisprudence'. Furthermore, one has to add: conversions may determine the structure of the narration although they remain fragments of the latter.

3.3.1 History Made, Given, Transmitted

How can we understand this complicated issue? In other words: what determines the relation between ourselves as a knowing and knowledgeable subject, and its histories profiled in narrations, which include conversions?

A first observation points at the stringent intertwining and historicity of all components that constitute a human life: even before a human being can begin to rethink, it is confronted with being lost in what happened to itself and its predecessors, its culture and globe included.

A second, immediately perceivable, insight is of direct importance for understanding the effects and importance of conversions. There is no point zero from which thinking (and certainly not rethinking) can unfold—our thoughts are born out of confusion and disarrangement and never out of any clarity.

Both observations prove almost intuitively the primordial role of conversions. Their task is *not* to create neutrality, clarity or cleanliness in view of preconditions of thought processes, but to provide *meanings* in the midst of confusions and historical criss-crosses *so that the flow of history never ceases*. Any contemporary physicist will agree with the conclusion that no meaning exists beyond human thoughts and natural phenomena that belong to the totality called 'cosmos'. A jurist as well as an historian might become overwhelmed by strange feelings and moments of uncertainty when he or she considers this implication of the effects of conversion on his discourse and discipline. And so will the philosopher and the politician.

However, they are not the only ones, and certainly not the first ones to experience this complexity in the profile of a human's knowledge patterning. Karl Marx wrote between December 1851 and March 1852 a famously critical text on the request of his friend Joseph Weydemeyer who started in New York a political weekly, entitled *Die Revolution* in 1852.[12] Marx's text refers to solely one day of the French Revolution, the 9th of November 1799 (French Revolutionary Calendar), when the first Napoleon Bonaparte made himself dictator by a *coup d'état*. He describes two commentators of the same events, namely Victor Hugo and Pierre-Joseph Proudhon. Hugo "confines himself to bitter and witty invective against the responsible producer of the coup

[12] Marx (1973) Vol. 8, 115. Engl. Ed.: Marx/Engels Internet Archive 1995, 1999.

d'état. The event itself appears in his work like a bolt from the blue. He sees in it only the violent act of a single individual." Proudon, understands the coup d'état "as the result of an antecedent historical development. ... He falls into the error of our so-called objective historians". Marx states: "I, on the contrary, demonstrate how the class struggle in France created circumstances and relationships that made it possible for a grotesque mediocrity to play a hero's part."[13]

This is an example of how critical thoughts concern day-by-day conversions in political options and meanings: the flow of occurrences that finally bring Napoleon to his throne seems an almost endless reordering of opinions, meanings, ideas, viewpoints, vested interests and political positions. But conversions that convert the basic concepts of the society remain undiscovered. Marx does not precisely formulate what finalizing master-conversions are at stake during the mass of conversions that compose the flow of social occurrences he criticizes. Disorderly conversions take place at every possible social level. Keep this conversion-directed description in mind, when one experiences with Marx that conversions are only considered as being completed and functional when they are successful—one could say: formed a specific attitude. Such awareness about framing and influencing, shaping history and dissolving from history seems to still be effective in today's legal and political actuality. Indeed, time is loaded upon all essential moments of experience.

3.3.2 Contract and Conversion

Law and its functionaries are confronted with the methodological reality that a discourse makes a component function in a wide lingual context but a conversion makes the same function in another context. The jurist in our days thus respects forms of equality and equilibrium to convert socio-cultural issues and themes via the creation of a context of enforceability connected with personhood to make those ideas legally applicable. An Occidental tradition provides a foundational example of jurisprudential conversion: the contract. The concept functioned for several centuries as the basis for a most general and fundamental legal qualification of human relations in state and society, linked to fragments of man's profile accepted by law, religion and politics alike. But the latter observation effectively veils, that even within the discipline of law various narratives can dominate with different chains of conversion as their basis. That seems to be the case in *contract*.

There are two narrative structures in the domain of law and legal discourse bearing the name *contract*: lawyers speak about contract in the *common law* (most clearly profiled in Anglo-American law) and in the *civil law* tradition. Two traditions; two profiles composed of the same narrative material; two discourses; two theoretical outlines; two types of social practices both named 'legal'; two regions on the globe with each a distinguishable socio-cultural background, history and outline of a future; two

[13] https://www.marxists.org/archive/marx/works/1852/download/pdf/18th-Brumaire.pdf, p. 2.

inquisitorial systems embracing the function of an examining magistrate. Both traditions are to be understood as *chains of narratives*, in each of which conversions take place to keep the narrative function. In both is *contract* a matter of agreement—in other words of a specific qualification of social interaction by means of legal meanings. The basis of this particular qualification is a social activity, often named 'mutual recognition'. As a consequence, one has to conclude that the term *contract* concerns a specific social form and value, which is not possible apart from acknowledged inter-subjectivity and structured on the basis of a social process known as 'mutuality'. Both *common law* and *civil law* are within the framework of these two narratives exploring appropriate manners to legally qualify human activities. It is at exactly this point that relevant conversions diversify in their relation with the different narrative structures.

The *common law* partitions the legal formatting through distinguishing (1) actor[s], (2) basis of action, and (3) object[s]. The actors are legally interpreted as bearers of rights and duties, as parties, resp. subjects in fields of action; the basis for their action is in most general terms qualified as 'exchange', whereas the objects at stake in the legal qualification are goods, services, capital etc. in the hands of the subjects. All those determinations focus upon a possible *breach* of contract, that is ultimately: upon a specific act or field of activities de-structuring inter-human mutuality. The judge has to deal with the latter, the de-structuring act, in order to make legal meaning function in view of these de-structuring powers unfolded by the subject. This clash of meanings (legal vs. subject) is the operational field for meaning conversions, as subject and judge both will recognize.

The narrative of the *civil law* focuses for its formatting on a specific human property called *obligation*. There is no individual that has no obligation in life—no matter how luxurious or deeply engraved in poverty the human being might be, in what cultural or social circumstances it may live, in what socio-cultural context its history is anchored or its present situation engraved. Obligations are human traits: one cannot deny any aspect of them, and thus do they form the basis for any possible legal qualification, which in its turn enables the lawyer to make obligations enforceable in law. They are a clear focus for conversion activities. Obligations as a human feature are also the basis for organizing *rules to be applied*—rules can never be individualized, always bear a social character and are fit to be socialized even by legal rules. It is the legal bond, to perceive and to experience in inter-subjectivity all around, which forms the basis of *civil law*'s emphasis on rule that organize rights and duties among individuals participating in social life. Conversions are in the view of *civil law* solely acceptable if they focus on that bond. At this point unfolds their full importance for the *civil law* thought patterning. All legal as well as philosophical issues have to respect this point of conversion's focus, civil lawyers presuppose more or less silently. Their silence is mirrored in the fact that there are no singular terms or concepts that point at conversions in any theory of law. Judges have to deal with infractions of the outlined legal bond, their ideas concerning a possible breach of contract are an instrument to safeguard the bond.

Conversions endured and caused changes in culture and in language. They do not reestablish their own origin; they do not offer insights into a first conversion on the basis of which we can convert today a proper and just, adequate and acceptable meaning. Was the term *contract* once obeying such demands? Nobody knows. But the chain of conversions escapes the logics of human history; narrations stemming from times in which a language did yet not have a grammar or syntax do the same. The latter illustrate the logic of history in senses and meanings that fulfill a hermeneutic role in our understanding of social complexities: they did in the past and do so in actuality—even deeply engraving into digital typologies of language and culture. All in all, it could become understood as a complex symbolization: the first conversion, from what into that, escapes from our perception and experience in the form of a narrative.

A narrative is never *only words*—it is always incidental and presenting its own pre-history, its own origin in multiple forms of otherness. But today's almost global structuring of narrative utterances has fundamentally changed since the last decade of the 20th century, especially since the introduction and global acceptance of all features of digital communication. That change was accompanied by a further diversification of conversions. Its particular character, to be read as 'referring to *legal* texts', became more important than ever.

3.3.3 Diction is Narrated Conversion

Conversions are *not* completely determined by words, expressions, concepts, terms or other comparable lingual occurrences. That is clear from the Ancient Greek's transition (towards Dionysian performances and their inherent speech events) to Marx's critical prose analyzing a day from the French Revolution, and since his texts to our days. This leads to insights on meaning and dynamics of *diction* in jurisprudence.

A central thesis of this Brief is, that conversions will be interwoven in narratives in order to be effective. One should add immediately, that conversions *change* narratives in the course of times like all other linguistic components. Those changes pertain to internal differentiations of for instance grammatical, syntactical or dictionary character, as well as to the traditions that master speech events in all variant social contexts, among which Court sessions and their judgments are an outstanding example for law and legal thought formation, as for instance UK legal traditions illustrate. Moreover, they seem to be influenced by the fact that the concept of a *narrative* in which they fit as if by nature, changed in the last decades—a change rather accompanied by a further diversifications than by any clarification of conversions. This illustrates that conversions are much more encompassing than those in use in our contemporary digital culture and techniques.

Indeed, conversions need narratives like the latter need the first. But any analytically fruitful awareness of conversions and their influence on meaning and sense directs to specific narratives at stake. These are changing in periods of time and thought. Exactly those processes of change in narrative structures, directing conversions to where they are needed most, seems the well-understood basis of modern knowledge, its sciences included. All conversions are relevant for a human existence, which is so vulnerably depending upon perception processes and on being perceived.

To exist is one thing, to be perceived another: that sentence could be remembered as basic for the intertwining of narrative and conversion. It is also foundational in times of change—in particular changes of narratives. Not only our words changed; they never changed first! It is the inner structure of our narratives that was converted during the final decades of the last and the first of our actual century. A word is submitted to its narration, one could conclude, and that insight profiles conversions. This change of narrative is not clearly perceivable in artificial languages, in professional or literary narrations but clearly in so-called folk tales, narrations of everyday in the midst of which we live and seem to understand reality. In that lingual context we think and rethink, diagnose and grasp meanings, embrace senses and commands, for short: in them we breath! They are the stories in which essential fragments are transposed from life to life and evidence to evidence—filled with inner wisdom directing the path in life to walk. Exactly because of this inner wisdom did the Brothers Grimm collect stories, did Flaubert include many in one biography named Mme Bovary, was Dostoevsky fascinating his readers while textually approaching sentiments and opinions of men and his readers. Leonid Grossman saw Dostoevsky as the inventor of an entirely new novelistic form, in which an artistic whole is created out of profoundly disparate genres—the religious text, the philosophical treatise, the newspaper, the anecdote, the parody, the street scene, the grotesque, the pamphlet—combined with the innermost structure of an adventure novel.[14] The Whole was the novel, not spoken words or constructed narrations.

We read the latter as precious literary objects, but they are in essence *means of communication*: documents witnessing changes of our own history and its patterns of understanding. No standards of beauty and artistry are at stake, but standards pertaining to the maintenance of our Self. Read a Daily Journal from 1980, one you could have been reading as a kid: you'll encounter titles that are never printed anymore—because they are forbidden or out-fashioned, not done or beyond boundaries of manners and morals. The same is true for words, images, drawings, photographs and the like. They are altogether elements of an expressivity, which is directly connected with changes initiated by conversion activities.

Note, how 'strong stories' (also called 'hard narratives') became fashionable. Such a strong story is a narrative, which at a first glance looks exorbitant and implausible. It does not present itself as the only truth possible but it opens ideological horizons and unfolds infinite political possibilities. It is a narrative that answers cool and distanced to many of the secret desires of an unknown and immeasurable public. It suggests providing directions in a disorderly world without taking the control of truth-values, ethical or moral dimensions seriously. The components of strength of the narrative are *not* those of securely reproducing facts or truthfully telling what happened. The distance to those categories is the strong narrative's strength. A strong story is not a story that tells exactly what has happened but a story that tells what happens according to the storyteller or the speaker—in his or her interest, to confirm

[14]Grossman (1925, 174).

her or his viewpoint or social position. It does not report facts but creates through story-telling facts that occur and function in other narratives.

Presenting a truth is a tour de force. They are effective in communication and illustrate an enormous power of connectivity, often supported by digital media. Hence the poverty and inefficiency of 'fact-checking' or the politics of datafication, which could require that 'data' and 'truth', or 'correctness', are close friends at least! This is of essence concerning the strong story: these narratives tell their story on what is offered as 'data' functioning as the narrative's foundation and its call for attention, consideration or policy. The strong story resp. narrative is strong and forceful because of the data considered, that is: thanks to the social process of datafication. Criteria of correctness are left to the hearer and his or her associated friends, not to the speaker who tells the story.

All this fits to a growing fear and uncertainty, caused by digital thinking and activity, in which connectivity is more important than communication. The main issue is to receive the message, the story—no matter whether you are (there) or not.[15] No wonder, that after a collective fear for a nuclear war, a desire for strong stories is at stake as a major issue of today's mental health care. Focus is on what the neurologist Oliver Sacks described as his nightmare: the human individual as continuously absent and only socially alert via his or her smart phone, all-consuming and solely directed towards a here and now. The 'homo digitalis' is in his eyes a gigantic neurological disaster: the truth of facts or the shame of fake news is pushed aside—perhaps the greatest conversion we experience in the third decade of the 21st century.[16]

In order to acquire an insight in the dimensions of that communication/connectivity, we note some different but altogether problematic issues: the *multilingual* character of new discursive patterns, the *multiplicity* of participants to consider, their *plural reality-awareness* and their embracing of a '*homo digitalis*' profile. All these traits of modernity are linked to 'multiculturalism', a main feature of *a society, which is composed of groups with predominantly different ethnic, geographic, religious and cultural roots and strive for equal positions on the markets of labor, goods and capital.*

Any understanding of a multicultural society requires a constant socio-political weighing of *difference* against *equality*. To perceive the other, to see the other as an equivalent self, to see the other as a source of my own identity, to accept his figure as a value in my inner self, to enjoy the wealth of the 'non-me', are forms of being an accomplished multicultural self. 'Active citizenship' comes into being only when I succeed to develop this *inner-directed basis of multiculturalism.* It is reflected in the evaluation of language. Acquisition and use of language reflect most clearly the emergence of an identity within the life of a self. Multicultural contexts challenge us to perceive, learn and speak more than one language. Any native tongue represents by definition a self amidst others and represents challenges to transcend the limits of that particular self. Listening to others implies the question "why is culture plural and not singular?" One has to find the answer to that question within

[15] D'Ancona (2017, 23, 41–61).

[16] Sacks (2019).

one's lifetime and lifestyle. There is an answer to propose: "because plurality brings harmony, which is impossible in the singular!" So, the multicultural self not only accomplishes recognition of plurality within itself, it also performs the task to pass legal and administrative discourse on to the discourse of civility, the discourse of tolerance at the communicative and democratic levels of social life.

It means, that one has to highlight the inner politics of the self for maintaining a self in social life. It is embedded in the philosophical adage that one has to be attentive to each fragment of the inner dialogue, which constitutes a human person. In that very special narrative we cherish the plurality of the "I", select what we include and exclude to belong to "us" and how we shape our judgments in that innermost area of our self-consciousness. All this is externalized in language. The expressions we use and the language we exploit bear the marks of our personal responsibility for that externalization process that "we are". The "right to use our own language",[17] bestowed upon us, must lead to break the immurement of shaping our life solely in our own language. In other words: one has to learn more than one non-native tongue and thus prepare in an exemplary manner for dialogues with those who embrace different values, norms, expectations and life styles. That is indeed a new dimension reaching beyond law and legal discourse: no life is possible and no entitlement of being an individual is justified without any personal practice of multiculturalism. One of the perhaps most important fields of that experience is embedded in the close ties between digital thinking and the unfolding of a human Self in a digitally featured society. The Self in digital contexts acquires its proper determination by means of connection processes, i.e. in essence without communication and thus without the characteristics that are typical of commonality, resp. the human warmth of a deeply understood togetherness.

Its default example is in today's Social Media activity, in which the message was send without consideration of any specific receiver. The centuries-old Speaker-Hearer Model became in digital communication a subtle, effective and powerful *formal* model without human content, that is without any consideration of linguistic or other human qualities of a Sender or Receiver, an 'I' or 'You'. The degrading of communication, visible and audible in conversations all around, leads to the progressive emptying of the Speaker-Hearer relations. Consider, how fate and future of modern man *are concentrated on the Self*—a name, an indication, a term, a concept that will often be disqualified as old-fashioned, as belonging to thought patterns of a passed-by century and thus as unfit for modern thinking, especially for digital culture. So the Self seems a central issue in the case of all social diction—jurisdiction not excluded! No, this does not concern any 'I' or 'You' in the sense of the dialogue as discussed in the midst of the past century. The issue that influences patterns of social existence and thought formation is truly distanced form dialogical settings and appreciations pertaining to whatever kinds of otherness. Conversions performed their task: they converted from the dual consistence of a polar 'I' and 'You' (maintaining even the classical Speaker-Hearer relationship) towards a thorough systematization of Sending and Receiving as extremes of an ideal connectivity digitally understood.

[17] See *Official Journal of the European Communities*, 25.07.94. Doc C 210/528 and 529.

The unanswered question is: what conversion changed our sociability and its world? There is one component in that question, which remains fully silenced and will also not be awakened by any lawyer today—if a specific type of conversion can be found as the case for these changes in the 'I', the 'Subject', the 'First Person Singular', will there be another conversion lightening up at the horizon of our research and rethinking? In other words: is the chain of conversions endless, delimiting time and order, terrestrial as well as cosmic dimensions? Are conversions in that regard different from other components featuring human life?

The question "what kind of conversion creates the actual human Self?" has unforeseen and perhaps also unforeseeable implications. An answer to that question is therefore widely beyond our capability of rethinking what has been though in law and related sciences—digital knowledge included. Only *social* effects of conversions are observable, and from those effects can some consequences be formulated. One is, that conversions became practiced and less intensely studied since the global embracing of digital techniques and attitudes. Living in an age of information became the new normal. Not only are data gathered, haunted or (to use and old-fashioned expression) documented[18]: datafication became the new passion. Indeed: conversions are like translations—but they are not. Conversions are like changes of- or even plays with words—but they are not. Conversions are strong or soft—but they are not. Conversions suggest to be grasped like an essential form—but they are not. Conversions show their faces everywhere—but we do not perceive them. They changed us from Speaker to Sender—but we are not aware. They changed us from Hearer to Receiver—but we are not aware. *What actual form will awaken us?* The answer is not heard: law and changes of its thought patterns will do—but: are we aware? Are we prepared to become aware?

The actual conversions challenged or even threatened our Self. Are social media able to perform without destructing the privacy of our Self? The answer of most users of social media is: 'I don't care'. Political problems with social media's *privacy* bother representatives in European Parliament or in a US political Party, but life goes on as if those issues don't exist. The "I don't care" seems to protect the Self without knowing what Self is at stake. The Self-determination of the Self, that are supported by social media has lead to multiple and often limitless notions of the Self. They embrace a loss of place, time and date like the Selfies made when and where a Self visits its world. Is there still a nature of thought and thought patterns, of observable and clinically relevant problems pertaining to consciousness or mind and cognition, sociability and communication? Are conversions belonging to the darkness of radicalism in global and climate sciences, in feminism or related manifestations of a Self that is no longer interested in clarifying limits of it self? Is there a climate change or a parallel crisis in law's diction because the Self of that diction seems endangered in multiple conversions?

---

[18]Blackmann (2019, 87 ff).

References

Balkin, J. M. (1990). The Hohfeldian approach to law and semiotics. In *Miami Law Review*, XLIV Florida, USA.

Blackmann, L. (2019). *Haunted data. Affect, Transmedia, Weird Science*, Bloomsbury Academic, London, UK.

Broekman, J. M. (2017). Street as Theorie. In S. Marusek & J. Brigham (Eds.), *Street-level sovereignty. The Intersection of Space and Law.* Lexington Books, New York/London.

Calvino, I. (1974), (1997). *Invisible Cities*, Harcourt Brace and: Vintage London, Chapter 4, *Introduction* and § 4: *Thin Cities.*

Calvino, I. (1974). *Invisible Cities*, Harcourt Brace & (1997) Vintage London, UK.

D'Ancona, M. (2017) *Post truth. The New War on Truth and How to Fight Back*, Ebury Press, London, UK.

Grossman, L. P. (1925). *The poetics of dostoevsky*. USA: Bobbs-Merrill Co.

Haan, J. I. de (1916). *Rechtskundige Significa en hare toepassing op de begrippen 'aansprakelijk, verantwoordelijk, toerekeningsvatbaar'*, W. Versluys, Amsterdam, Netherlands [No English Version available].

Hohfeld, W. N. (1919). *Fundamental legal conceptions as applied in judicial reasoning*. New Haven USA, London, UK: Yale UP.

Hohfeld, W. N. (1964). *Fundamental legal conceptions as applied in judicial reasoning and other legal essays*. New Haven, USA, London, UK: Yale UP.

Lewis, F. P. (2009). *"Tolerance, Pluralism and 'Fighting Faiths'" in Wagner/Bhatia: Diversity and Tolerance in Socio-legal Contexts*. USA: Explorations in the Semiotics of Law, Ashgate, UK.

Marx, K. (1973). "Der Achtzehnte Brumaire des Louis Bonaparte" (1852). In *Karl Marx/Friedrich Engels Werke*, Dietz Verlag, Vol. 8 Berlin Dld.

Maturana, U. R., & Varela, F. J. (1988). *The tree of knowledge. the biological roots of human understanding,* New Science Library, Shambhala, Boston & London.

Padel, R. (1990). Making Space Speak. In J. J. Winkler & F. I. Zeitlin (Eds.), *Nothing To do with dionysos?*. USA: Princeton UP.

Padel, R. (1992). *In and out of the mind: Greek images of the tragic self.* USA: Princeton UP.

Pencak, W. A. (2009). Race, class and the Supreme Court. In: Wagner/Bhatia (Eds.), *Diversity and Tolerance in Socio-legal Contexts. Explorations in the Semiotics of Law,* Ashgate, UK; USA.

Pickard-Cambridge, Sir A. (1953) (1991^3). *The dramatic festivals of Athens*, Clarendon Press, Oxford UP, UK.

Sacks, O. (2019). *Everything in place*. New York, USA: Knopf.

Schorske, C. E. (1981). *Fin-de-Siècle Vienna*. New York, USA: Vintage Books.

Wirth, M. (2011). Semiotics of parenthood in legal perspective. In J. M. Broekman & F. J. Mootz III (Eds), *The Semiotics of Law in Legal Education*, Springer, Dordrecht, Netherlands.

Chapter 4
Jurisfiction

Abstract The meanings of what we understand as law are the product of communication, togetherness, or social activity in whatever type of language—but in all types of coherence: a narration. From traditional legal hermeneutics to contemporary legal semiotics is law regarded and disregarded as embraced by discourse. With and within that discourse, narrations play the dominant role. They form a specific unity in a culture, so that partial discourses in law can form together a master discourse or narrative. This Brief's basic view is that the latter are the result of continuous and intertwining conversion processes. Elements of law's language, like 'form' or 'fact', are in essence the product of narrative contexts. That puts their 'fictional' character in perspective and determines their values, truth functions and related social qualifications. The narrative scope of law includes various types of language, in particular the analog and digital in modern language.

4.1 Form and Fact in Legal Thinking

The recent fashion to loudly debate "fake news" and "fake facts" and permit "fact checking" as a "fake control" is a clear *sign*. It tells us that traditional legal hermeneutics, the art of interpreting and architecting legal facts, is no longer a single means to articulate law's diction. That consideration leads the rethinking of legal thoughts towards a different background—an attitude articulated in the word "jurisfiction'. The expression 'fiction' is often mentioned in legal practices and became in the 20th century a reliable cornerstone in legal theories, for instance those on legal personality. But today has the theme been broadened and does it not only concern the *forms* of legal thinking but also the *facts* created by that activity.

Note, that "form" and "fact" are terms in law, which could precisely indicate a general crisis of the word in modern multileveled culture. These terms acquire a broader and deeper meaning and sense in the context of conversion jurisprudence and the observation that *conversions need to be interwoven in narratives in order to be effective*. This throws a surprising light on the properties of all types of conversion. 'Form' and 'fact' are today the most intriguing issues in the context of law and its discourses, but there have been others in classical hermeneutics and there will

J. M. Broekman and F. Fleerackers, *Legal Thoughts Convert*,
SpringerBriefs in Law, https://doi.org/10.1007/978-3-030-43517-2_4

still be others when digital thinking has deeper intruded law's narratives. The three: form, fact and conversion should be studied in their intertwining that creates legal thought patterns. The term 'jurisfiction' indicates this newly designed understanding and focuses on problems of recent hermeneutic profiles in law. They underline that there is no law or any lingual context of a lawyer's activity, which is not incarcerated in the basic structure of a narration. Lawyers are indeed, this Brief suggests, not sufficiently aware of this fact-creating fact, which determines the innermost norm of their profession whilst dissolving the dichotomy of form and fact as law's most constitutive feature.

That situation is even more complex since the majority of participants in actual legal conversations are characterized as 'homo digitalis'. Is the digital culture their most embracing narrative? The movements of their hands, filled with the little box named smart phone, indicates such an all-embracing mind or body. Law's actors seem to be never alone, always connected with information of all sorts, having information available through the small screen of their phone, reading and speaking governed by the images provided as 'smart' and supported by a global system called 'social media'. What type of smartness that could neurologically be understood, is at stake? The answer relates to digitally constructed *connectivity* which functions as the master narrative of today's legal subject—and not to communication of persons with full awareness of togetherness. The 'homo digitalis' survives because *togetherness* is at distance to being digitally *connected.* Whoever identifies connectedness with communication, fakes or is faked.

Its default is in today's Tweet or other Social Media activity, in which the message was send without consideration of any specific receiver. That lacking consideration is a major feature of legal relationships. The centuries-old Speaker-Hearer Model became in digital communication a subtle, effective and powerful *formal* model without human content. It is without any consideration of linguistic or other human qualities of a Sender or Receiver, of an 'I' or 'You'. The degrading of communication, visible and audible in conversations all around, leads to the progressive emptying of the Speaker-Hearer relations—a model formalized in each human hand acting in Social Medium techniques. Oliver Sacks qualified this feature during the last period of his lifetime as an important neurological issue that will determine fate and future of modern man. He was not aware to discuss one of the major forms of today's narration. *Fate and future are concentrated on "the Self"*—a name, an indication, a term, a concept that will often be disqualified as old-fashioned, as belonging to thought patterns of a passed-by century and thus as unfit for modern thinking, especially for digital culture. So the Self seems a central issue in the case of all social diction—jurisdiction not excluded!

Conversions convert the dual consistence of a polar 'I' and 'You' and the classical Speaker-Hearer relationship into a Sending and Receiving Model as an ideal connectivity digitally understood. The question, which remains unanswered, is: what conversion changed this sociability and its world? There is one component in that question, which remains fully silenced and will also not be awakened by any lawyer today. This Brief challenges a burning question: if a specific conversion can be found as the cause for these changes in the 'I', the 'Subject', the'First Person Singular', will there then be another general type of conversion lightening up at the horizon of our research and rethinking? In other words: is the chain of conversions endless, delimiting time and order, terrestrial as well as cosmic dimensions?

Indeed, the Brief hears suggestions everywhere, and arguments such as: conversions are like translations—but they are not. Conversions suggest to be grasped like an essential form—but they are not. Conversions show their faces everywhere—but we do not perceive them. They changed us from Speaker to Sender—but we are not aware. They changed us from Hearer to Receiver—but we are not aware. *What actual form will awaken us?* The answer is not heard: law and changes of its thought patterns will do—but: are we aware? Are we prepared to be aware of this? What about *forms* and *facts* in an age of conversion?

The actual conversions challenged or even threatened the privacy of our Self. Are social media able to perform without destructing our privacy? The answer of most users of social media is: 'I don't care'. The "I don't care" seems to protect the Self without knowing what Self is at stake. The Self-determination of the Self, that are supported by social media has lead to multiple and often limitless notions of the Self. They embrace a loss of place, time and date like the Selfies made when and where a Self visits its world.[1] Is there still a nature of thought and thought patterns, of observable and clinically relevant problems pertaining to consciousness or mind and cognition, sociability and communication? Are conversions belonging to the darkness of radicalism in global and climate sciences, in feminism, queer studies or related manifestations of a Self that is no longer interested in clarifying limits of itself?

4.2 Digital Language's Influences on Legal Language

Indeed: those questions come to the fore when digital features transform basic elements of legal language. But one is urged to *not* ask 'how' they transform, and is afraid that an answer would cause problems by conversions at all levels. No, this Brief challenges the lawyer's questioning differently. He should understand that conversions are *a matter of understanding a special narrative*: the Self's narrative as it sounds, is read or heard among other selves in pre-formatted patterns of law and legal discourse. In that perspective and at that level is the influence of digital language on law most clearly detectable. It is technically not possible to provide a general overview of all digital features creating legal language today. They are too widely spread, too complex in their genesis and appearance, too intimately related with the dynamics of today's cultural values in which law has to articulate itself. But very different and often surprising or shocking themes illustrate the characters subjected to the complexity of the intertwining at stake. Their notification delivers an analysis of the general problematic character of law's language in modern times. We mention: (a) the sexual identification of the Self by the Self, (b) the meaning

[1] Storr (2017, 243), Petrilli (2013, 101, 180, 207).

and sense of the ongoing narrative datafication in legal discourse, (c) the progressing automation of legal diction and procedure. All three show their close ties with law's narration. These narratives focus on the subject of law and legal discourse; hence their vital interest in the process of analog anchored legal thinking as well as today's digitalization. At this level is the digital influence most clearly observable.

4.2.1 Sexual Identification of the Self

The almost proverbial rigidity of law and legal discourse, and the deeply rooted need for fluidity in the unfolding of a human life are traditionally opposed. This becomes clearly visible in what occurred over the last decades in the Western world to the sexual identity of an individual and how the law replied. The sexual determination of a human personality has never been an issue in which the Self had a say and yet were the legal consequences intensively debated in all-possible contexts of life. Was there, or: is there freedom, when the subject is left without expression? In other words: gender determination was never accepted as the component of a specific (for instance a legal) narrative! Nobody will deny that modern digital techniques and forms of communication determine life structures, experiences and legal consequences of a Self's sexual determination today. This is a difference with earlier ages of Western culture in which that determination was *not* a matter of narration but rather a decision founded upon a simple *binary* observation of corporeal nature, noticed by others and eventually documented in society. The male/female distinction was legally fixated and its dual character did not belong to any socio-political narrative. The issue could perhaps become a matter of psychological, even psychiatric care or intervention but nothing more than that. *Central was the binary character of sexuality, so that any relativity in that regard was absent.*

Modern developments in thoughts about human nature and existential positions changed those issues. Those changes are a matter of conversion. The latter show that even gender determinations are not a matter of a binary situation or any other fixated determination. The Self had to unfold a specific relation to its proper determination, either provided by others or acquired by itself. The desired fluidity did not fit to any binary choice. This viewpoint was extensively proportioned in digital media. Gender diversity was unfolding in emancipation movements, in the midst of the eighties of the last century striving for the recognition of trans-sexuality and transgender positions as valued tensions within the binary gender concept. Trans-sexuality was named in the medical DSM III terminology only in 1980 and in 1987 confirmed in DSM III R. The term was treated as if it concerned the boundaries of social order, as was the term 'transgender', and remained positioned mostly as a 'disorder'-term even in 1990. Years and dates are perhaps not—but such a worldwide-recognized code as the medical DSM is certainly a witness of conversion processes, which we seldom analyze. Only later was the expression 'trans-sexual' accepted beyond concept boundaries in LHBT rights and a free determination of others who placed themselves somewhere at the enlarging scales of gender identity. Today, there is no Self anymore without encountering the challenge to position that Self in that field. Fluidity of sex and gender rules as well as distance to the binary character of gender determination became in this light socially and morally evident only in the very last years of the 20th century. Eyes and ears of lawyers are still filled with noises and presuppositions of the binary feature and the many consequences of that feature, which go with sexual identity in law as well as in ethics or social sciences. The sometimes dark and widespread cloud named 'conversion' provides an example for a form of identity, which appears despite the humanitarian and anthropological resp. psychological importance of the phenomenon of sexuality in itself, still in the borderline areas of human experience and its freedom. What has a lawyer to say about his function or role in conversion phenomena?

This positioning, linked with many modern social factors such as privacy, sociability, rights concerning communication and the like, is a central and everyday-life issue pertaining to conversion in law and society. The power to convert is at stake, and in the hands of the self-positioning Self—hands filled with smart phones that relate directly to ≠ MeToo and related LHBT apps. The combination of analog and digital thought patterns and the power to convert an object of (digital) conversion are clearly in effect. The Selfie's Self indicates the digital means of gender determination, which is mirrored in legal language as well as in social media. The latter encounter continuously new words, such as heterosexual, homosexual, bisexual, transsexual or transgender sexuality. It seems that there is no position of any subject called 'Self' by itself, which is not involved in forms of conversion dominated by digital communication techniques. This should exemplify the intertwining of digital notions and forms in modern legal language in the heart of a human existence. And it exemplifies the power of conversion at work in the cultural treasure named 'sexual identity'.

4.2.2 Narrative Datafication

Legal data must be understood as narrative data, or: data of 'law as a narrative'. But that viewpoint does not fit to the influence of today's omnipresence of digital media. Note, that even those who accept law as exploring an *artificial language* seldom accept the consequences and understand legal thoughts as a *specific narration* and certainly not the actual digital features. The expression 'narrative' seems to be too free, and to be gifted with too little obligation or to neglect the inner structuring power of law which appears for instance in criminal law as one of its basic features. In other words: *can data stemming from a 'legal narrative' become appreciated as 'legal data' or even 'legal facts'*? Thanks to law being a specific narration one can follow certain steps in that story telling activity all around the globe *despite* certain differences that are underlined in for instance varieties in common- and/or civil law, law of Far Eastern countries or elsewhere. Generality determines patterns of follow-up in each story and even the discussions about meaning, sense or structure of the participants in those narratives have common traits that unfold unifying forces. So one may not be surprised that datafication seems today a major digital feature without answering the question pertaining to law's narrative character.

Although a full-fledged process of legal datafying is still at the horizon and the function of data units in law's practices at a great distance, one should not underestimate the importance of the thought patterns involved. If a legal judgment is seriously understood within the framework called 'narrative', then its uniqueness of being *legal* judgment is flawed and its contribution to the language of law changed. The judgment does in that perspective not only consider a certain person or a specific social situation called 'theft' or 'murder' or 'breach of contract'. It also becomes a specific means in the context of other judgments with the final end to change, proceed or obliterate a social situation influenced by the change of narrative.

Here we encounter the power of conversion again: that power challenges us to decide whether not *all* components of 'law as a narrative' change under the influence of the globally reinforced datafication of legal issues. When a legal subject, a legally acknowledged individual, a self in law, a legal posture or a momentary appearance of law's diction, a word or expression are forged into the realm of data—do they not change their character, property or appearance? Do they not because of the datafication process in which they become involved distance themselves from what is called the 'true task of law'? In other words: any datafication of legal facts might alienate the legal character of such data.

The influence of digital language on legal language is accelerating, and threatens to become one of the most essential problems for a legal thought formation of the future—thoughts already financially supported by the economics of (legal) datafication. The frontier zones of understanding data and the existence of their digital language was a step performed *after* earlier distinctions proposed and executed in linguistics and semiotics in the preceding century by De Saussure, Peirce, French structuralism thinkers and others who studied text and narrative. The signifier as different from the signified, the code as different from the message, the synchrony as different from the diachrony, unfolded such suggestions.

Today is a different image at stake. Operators of computers and networks, which use special data transfer protocol in order to contact other operators who in their turn contact other, are the players on the field. Special websites are created to perform that task, so that social values and viewpoints can be selected by means of constructing hardware and software to maintain e-programs and other communicative issues depending on data that are measured, collected, reported and analyzed to function digitally. The quality of relations between data and devices determines the computer process at hand, and the latter plays an influential role in the experience and unfolding of social values. There is no 'I' and 'You'—experience anymore, which blossoms by the qualities of life pertaining to the human being outside of the shadows caused by data-creation and the transfer of data. Indeed, legal datafication is not an innocent process without influences on the concretization of justice and equilibrium by means of law.

4.2.3 Automation of Diction and Procedure

Each lawyer, judge or plaintiff has a dream. It is their job to create particular speech events delimited by law as a master narrative and *not* to utter words, sentences and thoughts they produce. They would rather fulfill the role of a silent component than of a speaking leadership. Data and procedures are speaking loudly—why and what should they contribute? Do not forget that law and legal discourse are qualified as *social* discourses. Questions pertaining to the role of speaker or hearer are therefore socially relevant long before they enter the realm of datafied issues such as connections between acting subjects. Are legal data reshaping the features of law in modern social life? The lawyer's desire to have legal functions performed per automate is a clear *sign* of change in that regard. And changes take place!

Data entangle personal and public themes and positions; they do the same with human and technical issues, with emotional and cognitive dimensions of human existence. They challenge the common and the connected as they do break traditional views on reliability and logic. But they also challenge language. This challenge created by data focuses in particular on *legal* language: legal data, like all data, bear traces of human, technical, symbolic or imaginary narrations. Many of those traces speak out loudly and want to be heard from their position of imprisonment in data metrics. They narrate: while doing so, they emphasize the multiplicity of language. The latter property is experienced when language embraces multiple temporalities and forms of conjugation coming to life by means of conversion. The drives to define one's sexual identity by the Self was an example of such an experience. Disjointed speech seems a matter of accepting *specters* (the rainbow is a beloved expression in that context) as a way to master multiplicity.

The Self speaks in various temporalities, and the lawyer would equally do so. If he cannot as an individual person, then his desire for automation flares up, because that is a process, which unfolds beyond the actuality of the spoken word; automated word orders go on when speech events died out. They can immediately be recovered and actualized when reality requires the new awakening of the mind. Data reinforce the lawyer's desire to enter the many rooms in the luxurious house of the legal narration—also those who have not been occupied for a long time. They are there, and are there as data that enable reiterations of procedures and word orders with well-known effects. Automation, never without data, is a truly correct image of law's narrative. It suggests equilibrium and hides away the many uncertainties of word choices or logics of utterance. It deals with all kinds of social questions, reaching from crime to contract, from traffic to health care, from supermarkets to studies of will and intention.

There is an intense interlocking of the lawyer's presupposed desire to automaticity in law's diction and procedure on the one hand (escaping from the Speaker-Hearer situation) and the expanding levels of digital technology on the other. It is important to underline that the digital culture in contemporary society and its scientific developments spends more interest in the unfolding and social acceptance of Artificial Intelligence than in digital communication techniques. A.I. has a double face: on the one hand is A.I. applauded for its attempts to expand the technical qualities and abilities of computers and their devices that focus on a broadening of intelligence in the cosmos *tout court*. In that regard functions the concept of intelligence as a terrestrial contribution to cosmic processes. On the other hand contributes A.I. to an expansion of the strictly *human* intelligence through artificial channels, which will become automated and thus may be conceived as independent from the human brain. But the brain remains the major metaphor for all those processes of expanding intelligence! Human rationality remains the most wanted and required property. Thought patterns of law and A.I. share the same values to operate as criteria for their research and development. And there is more in common: the entire A.I. domain is, like Law and its thought patterns, a matter of the constructive human mind exploring itself—reaching beyond its own boundaries.

In that perspective is the rethinking of legal thought patterns a most rewarding spiritual activity. It becomes clear that the traditional patterns, which proclaim and are for their development based on the separation between reality and the virtual, no longer honor the activities of a human mind. This distinction has to be re-thought. *The real is understood as including its virtual dimensions and properties*. Lawyers experience in their contacts with the worlds of their clients how the virtual includes and seems to be based upon what in their legal discipline once was called real. The classical steadfastness of embracing the distinction between the two and using it as an all-embracing argument would become abhorrent in everyday legal practices. The difference between the real and the virtual is to be revised because of the socio-economic implications of the hyper-connection in which human operate worldwide. Even the poorest populations on the global, the people most in need of means to maintain a daily life, differ from those who survived earlier centuries thanks to the techniques who unite the real and the virtual. *Scarcity* and *abundance* are reevaluated and thus touch worldwide economic principles that were valid in the past. The lawyer meets different souls today. He or she will be engaged in different types of language that shake our trust in factuality and inter-human communication.

We are not only confronted with a climate crisis of the world but also with a global crisis in the climate of the word.

4.3 Speech, Text, Narrative

> The word is reciprocal and thus equal;
> it is relation and thus difference.
> It is the act of the speaker and the act of the hearer
> to separate what is inseparable
> and to fixate what is not lasting.
> The word is indefensible definiteness.
> G. Mannoury, 1922

We consider speech, text and narrative as fundamental components of law's language before we approach the central issue of all legal thinking and application, which is in analog tradition named: the 'art of legal interpretation' or 'legal hermeneutics'. The difficulty is, that the three are instrumental in that interpretative process, but also subject of it. Their double function excels in law as a narrative. It does philosophically highlight the problematic relations among reality and word—a component of all philosophical concerns about understanding and interpretation. It might seem bewildering, but the pure existence of ground-forms of language such as *speech, text* or *narrative* have their own a constitutive power to form or de-form a participant in legal language and thus in law.

But what about specializing means of expression and communication: are they not a privilege for those who have studied the matters at hand and speak the related jargon, so that their selection became a decisive factor of communication? Mind you: that is a specifically analog way of thinking, which does not hold anymore amidst the preferred social media that guide me on the Street. It means, that my smart phone enforces me to integrate my digital ways of life in questions of my full legal identity. No, it has not to do with the question whether you studied law, knows about law's jargon or acquired knowledge and experience within any fragment of legal discourse. The question of being law's partner through lingual criteria is in the first place a matter of language(s) itself: it continuously occurs within the patterns of language. Law's lingual participants are linked to three specific levels: (1) the level of speech events, (2) the level of texts, and (3) the level of narration.

4.3.1 Speech

The phenomenon of 'speech' confronts us immediately with a remarkable insight we must embrace. Law's lingual participants are mainly understood as *speakers*—an impression mostly related to the dominance of all linguistic activities by the since Hobbes so popular 'Speaker-Hearer Model'. This model flourishes in every opinion about speaking and speech, and it tells us: there has to be one who speaks, one who hears or listens, and a language in which this activity takes place. John Searle's famous term 'speech act' confirms the omnipotence of this model. However, the strong influencing of digital means and techniques in the second decade of this century reduced the influence of this thought pattern, which still wants to be omnipresent and omnipotent in law.

It is a great example of how a linguistic model influences, manages and determines the roles and identities of participants in a specific discourse. Note, how being a subject of law (a term more at home in Civil than in Common Law patterns) is enforced by this Speaker-Hearer Model. The Model directs the meaning dimensions of the particular language that features law and its discourse(s). *Speech* is a social *event* and participating in law means withstanding any exclusion of the linguistic features of law from this event! We therefore already mentioned: a spoken word needs not only a speaker but also a context; it needs another individual as hearer and with that entity a common world of life-patterns. Is the Speaker-Hearer model surviving? Participants in legal discourse are precisely determined within the boundaries of legal language; only within these boundaries, that is: only within the precise limits of law as an institution, can an application of laws, a resolution of disputes, a negotiation of legal solutions and their political profits or disadvantages take place.

4.3.2 Speech Capacity

The acquiring of *speech capacity* is the very first and perhaps most important and fascinating issue. What happens when the speaker takes his or her position with regard to a speech act or the speech event? How is the speaker selecting utterances to function in speech? He or she is by no means carrying a dictionary that guides a word choice according to the requirements of the moment. There is no word reservoir found in the brain that functions during intertwinements with other words spoken by other individuals. The art of speech formation is a dark art: one must perform the right way by coping with unknown forces. A speech situation and its social character do not always cause the right choice. How do we understand? What is observed in the speaker's situation parallels literature in general. In the case of the latter is an outcry of interest: the outcry about the author, very proximate to the speaker, is "that all literature is a product of translation", as Michael Cunningham suggested in his homage to literary translators in Brussels, 2011. His slogan repeated the 2004 Coppola film "Lost in Translation" or perhaps the 2006 Edward Willett novel *Lost in Translation.*[2] But is the speaker *lost* in words or lingual stuff before he can even speak out? Is his or her *self* no longer there when words are uttered? John Searle's explications of the speech act do not provide an answer. Related theories about social acts as lingual utterances emphasize with John Austin the *activity* but not the *origin* of lingual materials.

Our conclusion is clear: conversion processes involving the Self are omnipresent and create (or at least support) the exchange of language occurrences. Conversation is the product of conversion just like literature is the product of translation, one concludes. But it also implies, that we will never become perfect in speaking. We live from beings spoken about and expected to become involved in life towards beings that are considered to speak and maintain individuality. It means: in the evolution of language in the domain of the individual progresses from being spoken-to towards speaking—we (no matter whether in a speaker or hearer function) always speak imperfect, because there exists no perfection in this regard! This gives new dimensions to the remark of Georg Steiner, who stated that it might well be that an authentically monoglot consciousness is historically and culturally an exception. Lingual capacities have, thanks to the specific structure of the human birth process, a polyglot origin—even in one and the same type of lingual expressivity.

---

[2] Willett (2006).

4.3.3 Speech Effects

This is what speech unveils: even conversions do not re-create us—not as a speaker, a hearer, a writer or a lawyer, although they do change the outlook of our conversations, the meanings we suggest in our speech and the effects that speech creates. Emotions, feelings, uncontrolled utterances or fragments of lost memory: they all are converted into words. Those concern outcries as well as moments of conversation, which seem well reflected, thoughtful and rational. Whatever context is at stake, speech phenomena (which remain lingual events that occur beyond any Speaker-Hearer model) do not take away that *law's participants occupy solely positions determined by law's language*. The order of words creates social patterns and order and reflects the rooting of the participating subject. That rooting of a law participant unfolds beyond speech as a freely composed linguistic event. Its unfolding is not in *writing* but primarily in *reading,* particularly in reading legal texts will a specific order be effective—even if, as in law, there is a predominantly artificial discourse at stake. The visual dimensions of such a reading are important in a world of slogans, billboards, commercial signs and digital connections.

Conversions play an important role. They could be unveiled when we become aware of the innermost effective creation of metaphors in speech—often freely tried out, just thrown into the flow of reasoning, sometimes at moments of surprising geniality. Figuration is a deeply rooted phenomenon in speech, mostly based on parallels and comparisons among words and expressions. Conversions are also fruitful in neologisms, which are brought to the oratory fore by means of experiment. They should renovate meanings in specific settings as the fruit of hitherto silently considered attitudes—free and independent, as slogan or intuition becoming public. Speech performance is truly a rich and complicated process. But law's rules and orders are ties to master speech according to its own, often institutionally frozen utterances. Law's expressivity is seldom a public speech to perform, but rather a public phenomenon that requires following and obedience.

4.3.4 Texts

Is in *speech* the Speaker-Hearer model an important determining power deciding about the profile of the participant in law and legal discourse, the same force is active at the level of *texts*. Neither the Writ of the judges' legal claims nor the subtle formulations of the Codes enable any layman to freely and openly discuss with a judge. The dominance of the Speaker-Hearer model takes any freedom to speak away. This makes understandable that a defendant does not foresee extensive dialogues with Judges or during Courts sessions. And the inverse, a dialogue in freedom initiated by a legal functionary at whatever level, can also not be expected—he or she has to speak the restricted and institutionalized language of the profession. Any official "I say …" refers to authoritatively colored words. These play a dominating role in the contrasts between the various levels of texts in law. Words are determined, roles fixated.

Even that mark of a word does not reveal the differences between a spoken word and a text. There has never been a moment in Occidental culture like ours. Writing varies for us from pencil and paper to bic and bloc, from typewriter and fax machine to phone, from phone to smart phone and its apps, from phone to lap top and from lap tops to computers that have the writing of texts only as their minor task. In other words: never before has writing been technically differentiated and reaching out to the most distanced areas on the globe. Inhabitants populating the outer banks of the Amazon River use the same TV programs and smart phones as those who survive in the favelas of Rio de Janeiro. Never has writing witnessed such an adventurous choice of technical means spread over the globe. Never has it been so full of preconditions to be fulfilled as today, the third decade of the 21st century.

What remains, is the insight and experience that a *human environment determines texts* and the particular features they display—no other terrestrial or cosmic phenomenon does the same! The most important component of that environment, unveiled in order to understand the text, tells us primarily: every environment is by definition *significant*. That is the basis for its signifying power, which is also determining law. Do not forget: signifying is interpreting as well as creating meaning in general! Peirce noticed this open and infinite character of a text where he outlined how deeply an *interpretant* is involved when texts are present. Everyone and everything will, strangely enough, perform that task. Every text has an "interpretant at work", he underlines. And that interpretant is not solely the consumer of what has been written—it pertains to activities of writer as well. Any writer is reader, as any reader is writer, one must conclude.

The function of an interpretant is clearly marked by a specific profile: there are inherent parallels in texts, as well as comparative and analogical strings of reasoning, which altogether unveil a specific desire of each text wherever presented: a desire to identity. That desire is approvable in two directions: one is the unfolding of imaginary- and another of narrative structures that lead to the profiling of an identity. We experience differences in texts on the basis of those properties, which satisfy the text's desire. We are not, or at least seldom, aware that those differences are ultimately based on the continuous, ongoing and constitutive powers of conversion, which disclose texts as profiled. It is, because texts generate connections between seemingly unconnected things, which will be realized via conversions. The poet, the scientist, the police officer, the judge, the philosopher, the journalist, the IT specialist, the author of novels or detective stories—they are all indebted by conversion processes that make it possible for us, the hearer, reader, subject or object, citizen or governor, politician or police officer, to intertwine specified and profiled texts, which we even give a name: the novel, the poem, the thoughts. This insight leads to the conclusion that even institutionally defined and diversified texts (such as legal texts in law, like judgments, closing arguments, minutes and protocols, contracts and by-laws) can be characterized as the result of conversions.

Texts function as ordering powers that are in effect within a society. An important component is the ever-changing and continuously effective process of conversion. As was mentioned are these processes marked by a strong desire to create identity. Where do texts find this identity, or what authority grants them an identity? The versatile character of texts in law and legal discourse, which features any rethinking of legal thought patterns past and present, makes it impossible that texts as such acquire a more of less fixated identity. It becomes especially clear in law, legal practice and its thought formations, that texts by themselves do not create a stable profile—their stability and identity derives from their social status, ultimately from the power that manages their application. Texts in legal context are centers of meaning-application at various levels. That does not characterize modern times. The writing and its text are differently valued in Greek society than in earlier Oriental cultures, Deborah Tarn Steiner demonstrated.[3] This could be of importance for our modern appreciation of writing and particularly of text. In Ancient Greece writing emerges "as *a shorthand for the threat of autocracy*, (our italics) and its rejection of subordination a symbol of a nascent democracy in the Greek city-states... which belongs to the larger set of symbolic activities that distinguish the barbarian from the Hellene" she states. The Greek lifestyle brings new views into social action, which treat texts in different contexts in order to have them function in hitherto unknown ways. "The king so dominates his state", Steiner explains in the above quoted fragment, "that he has appropriated the defining characteristics of a popular regime. He is the polis, the domos, and the chief president of the boule, a position properly determined by lot. His dominion extends over his subject's private and public lives, and includes the hearth, which is both the focal point of each household and the symbolic city center for participants in the democracy. The king announces his will through the nod, the sign regularly given by human and divine tyrants to declare their consent. To reinforce its all-encompassing authority, the wordless gesture has claimed the apparatus of democratic procedure, the voting pebble that selects officials and concludes business in organs of popular government." Pelasgus' use of the adjective *eleutheros* defines the freedom of speech and action that citizens enjoy and contrasts with the rigidity of what is nailed, stamped or sealed. A fragmentary line of Pelasgus quoted at p. 168 (the name meaning ancient, the ancestor of the mythical inhabitants of Greece) clarifies also for modern man in our 21st century how

> the nail of this resolve has been driven in piercingly so as to stand fixed.
> This message is not inscribed in tablets nor sealed in the folds of papyrus sheets;
> from the tongue of a free man you hear it plainly

Indeed, the tensions between speech and text are often high in Occidental culture, from the Ancient Greek until our days. The Writ of the Tyrant might be in our hands filled with our smart phone or with our longing for the spoken word as a symbol of freedom in the lines of a poem. Herodotus used the term "I view, observe" [*theaomai*] to describe a seeing that takes in only eternal characteristics, which see the whole and not the part, and does not penetrate beneath the surface. Do we see, do we notice in what Steiner registered as being the Ancient Greek mania for recording and

[3]Tarn Steiner (1994, 127).

preserving information, which we call *datafication*? Indeed, a text has also in our days a deeply rooted political relevance.

This observation is the more important for law and legal discourse. Steiner's thesis concerns the authoritarian character of writing, so that each text is in suspect to represent and effectuate authority and power. Again must be underlined: not only what is written, not only the writing procedure itself, not only the reading each writing enforces, is of importance but always *the social role* the text is destined to fulfill is of essence and has to be checked philosophically. Legal texts are never free speech phenomena. They are orders, conclusions, dispositions, statue documents, contracts, codes or studies on law, legal dimensions and meanings to be respected, instructions to give texts an authoritarian function. They always refer to other texts in law; the network of their interdependency of specific meanings is in many regards like a digital network. Technicality, strictness of following prescripts, formulations that withstand doubt or in-depth consideration or the use of specific terms, words and meanings are the vast materials of legal knowledge and thought. Lawyers seem to respect that words, punctuation marks or sets of words are sometimes wiser than the author. The often-disputed distance to a deliberation or discussion of a legal specialist's position in everyday life is the result of the role legal texts are predestined to fulfill.

Those texts tend to become documents as soon as they might be discussed. Texts reporting histories, registers belonging to clarification attempts, catalogues of data and acts that are relevant for legal understandings tend to be filed, boxed, sheltered or digitally datafied. Documents are seldom available, only researches or caretakers enter their shelter or bring them to a specified home, for instance a library or museum. Often is only their reproduction available: the originals are protected as if they were a High Priest, a King or Emperor. Or, formulated less respectful, one could say: documents resemble people talking in sleep (Susan Howe[4]). A document, and certainly a legal document, should remain perfect by being perfectly what it is because you are not allowed to touch it. Indeed, law's text functions as a document—it is hardly believable in our age of phenomena belonging to a digital culture. One of the most hidden consequences seems to be, that the powers of *soft conversion* (i.e. the transference of meanings, thought patterns, styles, data etc. into other contexts without destroying the wholeness in which they function) are at the edge of becoming a specific technique of law and legal language. It seems to be never discussed: what is a conversion that had to loosen its ties with inspirations about the many meanings of life? Can a lawyer rethink his or her thought patterning so that it becomes successful in formulating an answer?

4.3.5 Narratives

Speech survives in texts, but texts based on speech pay often a high price—that price called 'fixation' is also to be paid by lawyers. But the situation of *narratives* seems

[4]Howe (2015, 62).

different from texts—narrations being an anthropological and socio-cultural phenomenon of importance. Whenever we speak, we direct ourselves to others, and that choice of direction already acknowledges the social structures and hence the patterning of our words: *narrativity* is at stake. In the narration are subject positions created through the application of linguistic categories, carried on by culturally inspired uses of words and phrases. The narration has its inherent structuring force and determines positions of participants, real or fictive, legal or (for instance) medical. Whether and how legal narration manages its thought patterns in that same manner seems a question of utmost importance for rethinking law's thought patterns.

Narration is on the one hand an important rhetorical mode of discourse, but on the other, at a completely different level of thought a most remarkable phenomenon, namely a specific *breach of silence* (i.e. articulation possibility). We are seldom aware of the fact that meanings of words spoken by ourselves reach deep into their proper pre-history and are confronted with their proper narrative origin and thus meet silence. Rethinking what we say sometimes touches what Peirce named a 'silence *before* breach'. It must be underlined that there is a difference between this silence *before* breach and any silence *after* breach. The first is created (a domain in which linguistic categories cannot fixate social structures) the second a matter of consequences of creation. It is clear: *with narration, 'meaning' steps out of silence* and thus becomes present in chains of signifiers with multiple layers of other meanings; it never fills out just one particular sign. Peirce would have underlined: a sign has no meaning— or it has access to and is supported by many meanings. Even a narrator tells a story in which he or she cannot decide. "Heaven and earth" is from the hypothetical days of Creation until our less-hypothetical days of the 21st century just a sign of multiplicity and multilayered articulation. Meaning, always process and awareness of otherness, is always something else, among which *silence*. A narrative is for that reason never *only words*—it is always incidental and presenting its own pre-history, its own origin in multiple forms of otherness. Are these thoughts a lawyer recognizes?

4.4 Towards a New Hermeneutics

The question is not nonsensical. 'Change' is the contemporary keyword for all our understanding. We reformulate: conversion jurisprudence leads to new insights into 'legal hermeneutics'—the art of interpretation. Those insights challenge the lawyer whose daily practices perform at all levels, but do seldom imply any theoretical awareness about this activity and its basics, in particular the profile of an individual lawyer. Interpretative statements occur today under the sign of *change*: they do not confirm what is fixated but focus on what is involved in a process of change. What lawyers judgingly interpret, changes the lives of a citizen, and those changes bring perhaps new rules to the fore, which are soon, and at various levels, qualified as 'data'. A new profile of legal hermeneutics seems actualized: stories changed, texts changed form and content, conversions interpret, and the master-narrative called "Speaker-Hearer Relationship" is no longer the basic model for lingual and other utterances.

Those changes form a uniquely new cultural phenomenon: the intertwining of different types of language and of conceiving reality: with an accent on the analog and the digital world. This situation creates a wealth of conversion opportunities, which form a central and yet overall power of meaning and sense in life.

So, one should consider the changing hermeneutics no longer as an individual attitude change, but as a cultural phenomenon in which the lawyer has an important role to fulfill. The legal function is no longer a matter of deciding among fixated elements of a textual or of any other lingual character, but rather of creating realities expressed in a plurality of language types. No wonder, that from one or another fixed standpoint the ordeal 'fictive' is heard. But that term itself received in these new cultural circumstances a variety of inter-changing meanings. This will be confirmed by the registration of particular alterations in the major components of hermeneutics: the legal texts became different, the jurist's act was broadened beyond the trusted linguistic model that supported the idea of interpretation, and the support of that model vanished. What are the consequences?

New insights in the actual dimensions of legal hermeneutics illustrate that the lawyer is no longer an interpreting individual but rather a conversion agent.

No, a modern lawyer is not profiled as a lawyer anymore because of his knowledge or mastering of recent legal rules and their textual anchors, but because of his membership: his being a conscious member of an ever-converting society in which he participates and knows to trace paths for himself and his companion citizens. This all-embracing change leads to questions concerning the totality of modern man in law. The lawyer and his or her client experience how intense conversion is their oxygen: no lawyer or client can unfold a truly human existence without converting life's components. Such issues used to be qualified in the past century as 'existential'. Indeed, one asks: what is an interpretation of a something that can no longer be understood as a text? And what if an interpretation unfolds by means of actions that are no longer an interpretation in the sense of understanding but of data? How to qualify distances to the dominant model that embraces the activity of a speaker and a hearer? Where are we? What do we learn from these changes, what do they tell us, and what is their meaning on our daily routes to our Selves? A newly forged awareness, one can answer, but how will our daily path expose the truth about us, their walkers? Are the hermeneutic changes not steps towards an annihilation of the Self, our most intimate companion in life? Such questions form the climate in which the rethinking of legal thoughts made the word 'fiction' a crucial element of hermeneutic concerns and a basic notion of what should be brought to an understanding for social life.

4.4.1 Stories Changed

Any consideration of law's diction is a matter of rethinking law as a fragment of culture. It is not just an exploration of specific words or utterances applied in a legal discipline. This forms the background of an important observation: legally relevant stories, those of law's formalities included, changed and today still change considerable. It means that stories resp. narratives are not anymore the subjects of *legal* hermeneutics in its traditional sense, which marked law (next to literature and religion) in the 20th century. And, what is more: this observation is valid beyond the boundaries between civil law and common law. Compare a story of Kafka with a series of Facebook pages, or be aware how US jurists momentarily cope with chains of Tweets from their President! Indeed, one concludes: the character of stories or narrations changed, not only their belonging to one or two types of language, and thus the subject of law's art of interpretation. They changed from literary (as the Grimm brothers made clear and one can read in later narrations from Kafka to Faulkner and deep into our modernity) to other forms that focus no longer on the communication of aesthetic and emotional criteria but on connectivity and forms of information and data exchange. Law has been thoroughly influenced by this change because an important domain of its discipline, *the legal text*, changed so that legal practices seem no longer to rely upon their classical art of interpretation. Contextualizing data is nowadays a form of interpretation, a form of loosing ties between fact and actual reality—indeed: not only forms and facts but also words of actual narratives have changed considerably.

All those changes relate to deeper cultural levels of meaning and sense. When the German philosopher Friedrich Schleiermacher (1768–1834) gave his lectures on interpretation of texts and speech (in Halle, Germany) he focused on the task of the interpreter to understand a text as well as and then even better than its author—a famous slogan, which has in its almost global application been understood as a psychological starting point of general understanding. One should interpret a text in relation to the mentality and development of the author before one pays attention to the language in which it is written. Note, that the first, psychological, component seems to be a key to the cultural embedding of texts via their author, whereas the language seems excluded from that chain of facts and factors to grasp the meaning of a text. The question parallels another famous theme, called the 'hermeneutic circle'. The latter tell us that we cannot understand a language, a person or a text without understanding its parts, but we can also not understand any part unless we understand the whole. The circle in which we are imprisoned is the continuous reciprocity between the whole and its parts. Has this viewpoint changed in the past centuries?

It is, in any case, a moment of cultural development known since the Ancient Greek. They struggled with oral and written texts, with oracles and myth, with philosophical and literary works effective in public and embracing important political consequences that colored not only the status of the immigrant and the citizen but also the laws and contracts all had to obey. A comparable complexity featured the Western Middle Ages, their religious and philosophical foundations in particular. No wonder that the first decades of the 20th century were still marked by the hermeneutic circle, that is: by the tensions between parts and the whole. Heidegger's insight concerned an ontological reality being the foundation for understanding the text in order to change its perspective as for instance formulated by Gottlob Frege, who stated 1884 that it is enough if the sentence as whole has meaning; also its parts obtain thereby their meanings.[5]

But a common position, undisputed since centuries, is at stake in understanding today's interpretation resp. hermeneutics. At issue is:

> The desire to understand, to know or to have insight in what the author of a text wanted to say, including his anchor ideas and eventually the preconditions of his existence as mirrored in his or her text.

That crucial position repeats the major structures of the infamous "Speaker-Hearer Model", which dominated all thinking about speech, text or language in the ages of analog language. It did form the basics of our understanding and interpretation of written or spoken meaning and sense. Deviations from truth and trustworthy regions were inacceptable, socially problematic and ethically condemned. Today's revaluation of facts and fictions as facts implies a step outside the SH Model and embraces those steps as possible components of a narration. The latter is no more a product but rather a socio-cultural context of the human power to understand and interpret reality and language created by a human individual functioning as producer and narrator. 'Fiction' became an indication for a newly outlined hermeneutic approach, which accepts different narratives (texts and structures), interpretations (conversions) and models (other than the SH model).

This change has far-reaching consequences, especially if one considers the narrations that were the central issue in our understanding and interpretation of what one was reading and hearing in social contexts. The types of narration could apparently change as if they were changes in fashion, or in the ongoing self-determination of sexual identity. They became public processes, matters of connectivity to be deciphered and communicated in other terms, words and techniques. Three aspects should be mentioned:

(a) a narration is no longer performed with the ultimate purpose to tell the truth. *The* truth does no longer exist; *a* truth is only a perhaps functionally determined component of the narration, which is composed out of many meanings, senses, insights and perspectives.

(b) a narration is today always composed of two types of language: the digital and the analog language. Their intertwining is strong, and any narration qualifies the strength of that inter-connectivity as a major value of the story, resp. text at stake. Digital clues are for instance visible when the narration's components are treated as data and the story's data are judged by means of an analysis of the relevant datafication process of those constitutive data. Instead of listening to the opinion of a reader, one reads the results of analyses of datafication processes leading to the text or story: that is an example of actual digital intertwining of analog types of language and thought.

(c) a narration depends on more social qualifications than being a priori understood as 'a fairy tale', a 'poem', a detective story', a 'novel' etc. There is a long list of new story-types, which are socially, legally or politically relevant today. They

[5]Frege (1884).

are all implying different types and degrees of conversion that determine their composition and analysis. One particular type of narration is named the 'strong story', which is under our eyes or in our ears an indestructible moment that could have been provided by "an influencer" rather than "a story teller". It is not a story that tells exactly what has happened but a story that tells what should or will happen according to desire or insight of the provider. It does not report facts but creates through story-telling facts that can or will occur and function in future narratives. Their form is seldom a written page, a booklet or a journal—mostly a Tweet, a Facebook page or another marker of digital origin. Not only a Tweeting politician, also a Tweeting poet is imaginable today! The 'strong story' is therefore an example of how digital means broadened our mentality, described by Husserl as "attitude" or Goethe as "Stimmung" and qualified by Ezra Pound as "a news that stays new"—forms of reception of a narrative have always been like a psychic reaction. The digital culture brought us in that regard nothing unknown!

4.4.2 Interpretation Changed

This means: *the act* of interpretation changed, since there is no exquisite subject that functions as hearer or reader gifted with the key to someone else's meanings, attitudes and intentions. The more components of a narration are (or are treated like) data, the more is the art of interpretation involved in a process of change. The 'strong story' is an example of how the narrative itself takes the role of the narrator. The story can in that case only be understood if one is prepared to distance oneself from fact, fiction or truth as decisive values of the narration and its interpretation. The social structures of the process of interpretation and understanding are challenged fundamentally.

This is of essence in the strong story: they do not tell their story on the basis of truthful experiences, reflections, beliefs or convictions, but on what is offered as 'data' functioning as the narrative's foundation and its call for attention, consideration or policy. The strong narrative is strong because of the data considered, that is: forceful thanks to the process of datafication. Criteria of correctness are left to the distanced citizen, the hearer and his or her associated friends, not to the speaker who tells the story. The essence is: the story is no longer told, but (re)constructed, that is: managed in the context of datafication processes. Indeed: the *storyteller* became a *data manager*. Large sections of global economics demonstrate those implications; at a small and almost private scale is the same structure in effect for those who manage parts of their lives via social media. To judge along lines of 'falsehood' or 'fiction', 'fakeness' or 'truth' is no longer a value judgment but a sign of helplessness in understanding the occurring changes of hermeneutics.

4.4.3 The Speaker-Hearer Model Dissolved

All these changes are utterly important for understanding law and its discourse in daily life. The observations on legal language becoming an artificial language are in this light almost irrelevant. The worries about legal expressions and its language in general being incomprehensible on the street and thus failing to create the essential social contacts are also barely relevant. In how far is the legal subject incorporated in the data processing that is in part organized as 'modern law'? The distances at stake are often heartbreaking. All those considerations are encapsulated in the slogan that the Speaker-Hearer Model is lost in Western civilization, thanks to the intertwining of our analog and digital language, technique and pursuance.

Note, that this dissolution took less than half a century to occur: nobody knows what will be the art of interpretation (and legal hermeneutics) when other types of language and other styles of utterance developed. Dissolution of such an important model that formatted all modes of human expression for centuries raises such questions but does not answer them. Will law of the third decade in the 21st century become a discipline and discourse without interpretation (and thus beyond legal hermeneutics) and thus a social domain of technical applicability regarding default social connectivity? Nobody knows, but cultural changes seem to go that direction. It could appear to be a matter of mastering cultural forces and technical preferences to decide. The intertwining of analog and digital forces of expression appears to be a great challenge at the horizon of law and society.

The perhaps most hidden conversion at work in law can be discovered while studying the downfall of traditional hermeneutics and the dissolving of the Speaker-Hearer Model that was functioning through the ages. Here is a clear example of *the intertwining of narration and conversion*: the reason why we underlined the importance of the so-called 'strong story'. The thread of this occurring conversion in the deep layers of law and its discourse becomes perhaps energized by the empathy of the active lawyer for changes from interpretation to automatism. His or her empathy grows with every act that includes the use of a smart phone or the techniques of any other social medium. A loss of linguistic ability, a loss of ability to master words and expressions in speech events, supports this fundamental change in legal practice and law's thought formation.

To speak in law threatens to become the sending of a message, and the latter will in the forthcoming years be no more than a specifically prepared data transfer—perhaps fabricated by legal computer programs which are already imaginable in special legal sectors (such as economics, contracts, certain domains of criminal behavior, laws regulating traffic on the street as well as on the Internet) but are not available yet.

The threat of this conversion remains forceful in each legal act, and the domain of conversions in general seems on its way to characterize our jurisprudence in the coming decades. Only a team of specialists composed by legal assessors and theoretically trained IT-specialists, technicians that master connectivity as well as social scientists, which understand the many functions of a narration on the street as well as in parliament, could fulfill the task. Conversion jurisprudence may not yet be fully understood, but we are aware of its foreshadowing. The self-understanding of a lawyer might change, as law's hermeneutics did: the lawyer will no longer be the interpreting specialist but a conversion agent. Is a jurist of the future no longer the *homo sapiens* characterized by his or her careful interpretation and understanding, but rather a *homo digitalis* mastering complex conversion domains?

References

Frege, G. (1884). *Die Grundlagen der Arithmetik: Eine logisch-mathematische Untersuchung über den Begriff der Zahl*. Breslau: Dld.

Howe, S. (2015). *The quarry*. New York, USA: A New Directions Publishing Corporation.

Petrilli, S. (2013). *The self as a sign, the world, and the other. Living Semiotics*. New Brunswick, USA, London, UK: Transaction Publishers.

Storr, W. (2017). *SELFIE how the West Became self-obsessed*. London, UK: Picador.

Tarn Steiner D (1994) The Tyrant's Writ. Myths and images of writing in ancient Greece. Princeton, NJ, USA: Princeton UP.

Willet, E. (2006). *Lost in translation*. USA: DAW Books.

Chapter 5
Conversion Jurisprudence

Abstract No, the profile of individuals in the legal profession is not that simple. He or she is by no means just a conversion agent, or a *homo sapiens* losing traditional wisdom, or a *homo conversionalis*, a manager of behavior apps. Never an engineer of digitalized social fields, the jurist will not solely master specific social behaviors or become the manager of large-scale political fields of law in his role of a legal scientist. These suggestions are too simple altogether. They just bring the analog and the digital in opposition and with them the many other profiles of culture that determine modernity. No, *not an antipode*, this chapter argues, *but a continuously changing integration* opens up to other and more interpretative views on reality at stake in this Brief! That is also the legal field—in particular its individualistic traditions. With integration evolves the profile of the mediator, his or her specialism and the requirements of lawyering in general. This type of intertwining directs us. We focus on law and its functionaries as a never-ending process of change in all domains of culture, which marks the 21st century. It concerns the riddle of wisdom and automatism combined, of individual privacy and social fixations together, of philosophical considerations and the coercion of conversion integrated.

5.1 Jurists in Contemporary Culture

Conversion became, thanks to a globally intensified communication, a key-activity in nearly all fields of thoughts, sciences and social life. It is absolutely no exception to mention jurisprudence as a field influenced by its problems, insights, forces and requirements. Money, measures or weights are to be converted, but also words, insights, values and opinions as well as judgments and provisions. Conversion is part of the moving of the world of everyday and so it touches all our lives, their legal dimensions included. As a consequence, conversion intrudes everybody's existence everywhere—not only in professional roles but also in a majority of private aspects of life. Facts offered in real life situations are nearly always embedded in the mainstream of conversions. Viewpoints and opinions undergo the same fate. Yet, there is a difference between the presence of digital communication and the presence of conversion powers. The first is like a cloud over our daily life and its entire cultural sphere. The

J. M. Broekman and F. Fleerackers, *Legal Thoughts Convert*, SpringerBriefs in Law, https://doi.org/10.1007/978-3-030-43517-2_5

latter is understandable in a different manner: not only as a consequence of technical innovations and changes, but rather as seemingly anchored and appreciated in our continuously evolving social life.

5.1.1 Ego Involvements

Important fields of technical and scientific research and knowledge are available and spreading today: even deeply engraved in regions of human essence and behavior such as medicine, psychiatry or the forms of a private human life. They have an important point of departure in Immanuel Kant's *philosophical* impulse. He pluralized the inner structure of the human *ego* and spoke of an *Ichspaltung* (a *split 'I'*) in his *Critique of Pure Reason.*[1] He changed the awareness of our Ego as if he foresaw Freud's later practices and thus laid also foundations for an understanding (and above all a self-understanding) of the jurist and all who read law or are subjected to the law. His venture to pluralize the *ego* and understand various phases of its nature and effect as conversions challenged us in the 21st century to try to achieve knowledge of *unfolding philosophical considerations when reality is experienced* and its force we call 'conversion'. One could correctly formulate that Kant was the Occidental philosopher who generated a structured interest in what we call today the 'Self'.

It fascinates in how many regards this observation leads to a philosophical understanding of the problem of *an origin* and how this is relevant for our understanding of *conversions*. The concept of 'origin' seems foundational to human experience, and in particular to a widely reaching *self-experience* broadened beyond individual experience. Indeed, the Self asks where *the beginnings* of conversions are to be found. The answer is based on an understanding of the changes' architecture.

But the philosophical question is categorical: *is* there a beginning *at all*? Or do we awaken amidst our involvements in conversions—and then qualify them as a beginning? Edmund Husserl transferred the Kantian intuition during the first half of the 20th century into a foundational consideration. 'Phänomenologie' was his philosophical project marked by the classical feature of *beginning*. His major thesis was, that one acquires philosophical insight only *after* a change of attitude, that is: whilst awaking from the naivety of exclusively positive foundations of truth and reality. All this was, however, based on the (naïve) conclusion, that there exists "a harmony between the world itself, e.g. the truth, which are valid for itself, and our acts and forms of knowledge".[2] A link with conversion was never proposed. Husserl himself did not spend much attention to this topic but forwarded the term *Einstellung*, resp. *Einstellungsänderung*. He remarked that who "experiences the bristle of skepticism in a painful manner" and remains within the boundaries of the naïve-natural,

[1]Kant (1781).

[2]Husserl (1923/24) (Ed. 1956, 245).

should distance oneself from that experience—that was all![3] Continental as well as English-language studies on phenomenology did also not treat the *attitude-change* as a primary issue.

This conversion, Husserl repeated in an article on *Phenomenology* in the *Encyclopedia Britannica*, concerned the generally known change from a naïve towards a non-naïve attitude or the change from pre-reflective towards reflective, or naïve-natural towards non-naïve-natural views. We underline that his proposal was formulated in analog language, which embraced an individualistic framework. But the conversion upon which Husserl focused, unfolds in other directions: once the gap between naïve- and non-naïve attitude conquered, a new and in essence non-individualistic naturalness is presented as the first step towards a transcendental position. Note, that this position was qualified as the position of a 'transcendental ego'! After attitude changes from 'non-naïve-natural' character towards 'reductionist' attitudes, he outlines a position that does not embrace any individualistic attitude anymore: social features of life dominated and conversions envisaged 'totality' and/or 'wholeness' as their evident character. Husserl's 1929 lectures entitled *Cartesianische Meditationen* proved the presence of the constitutive power of social dimensions in the flow of conversions, a flow that was in Husserl's phenomenology understood as the product of the newly outlined attitude changes!

Such considerations are not only an outstanding example of recent Occidental philosophy. They also provide an insight in the global interest in understanding the meaning and sense of our continuously unfolding process of acquiring knowledge. We may experience the bristle of skepticism now and then, but we never know when and at what occasion that experience challenges us to definitively change position. Conversion covers it all. Life in a naïve-natural attitude is easy and warm (often too easy) and insufficiently demonstrating where limits are and damages could emerge. No wonder, that the downsizing and even reduction of that attitude is for Husserl the beginning of walking the path of philosophy. The latter should lead to what he calls 'humanizing the human' (Vermenschlichung des Menschen)[4] an awakening linked to this first step. The same was in the mind of the US philosopher Charles S. Peirce who remarked in 1903: "Possibly … Firstness is the embryo of being"). It was mentioned that this change of attitude is first a matter of individual personality, but already focuses on Wholeness and the Whole, and thus delineates Conversion in its innermost basic structure as a necessary next step.[5] Those who think of conversion in its religious meaning or refer to conversion as *metanoia* (thinking with another consciousness) are perhaps fascinated by Husserl's own formulation: "It may become clear somehow, that the complete phenomenological attitude … is first and in essence a completely personal alteration, which could be compared to a religious change…"[6]

Accepting a plurality of the *ego* is a first phase of conversion—the attitude conversion from naïve-natural to non-naïve-natural—and opens up to transcendental

[3]Husserl (1923/24) (Ed. 1959, 27).

[4]Husserl (1935/37) (Ed. 1954, 429).

[5]Broekman (2010, 37).

[6]Husserl (1954, 140).

positions in which the distinction between individuality and collectivity, the single and the whole, is put in perspective. This activity does not imply any positioning of the subject as the philosophical ground for thought formation: it rather opens up to *transcendental* positions. All this is not exclusively a matter of analog language. It is rather the domain of human expressivity as such and in its entirety, related with the acquiring of knowledge of matter, energy and reality. Next to analog types of lingual expression are the momentarily strong influences in effect of digital- and other types of inclusion. Indeed: human knowledge is a matter of wholeness—a wholeness concerning everything that can be understood as belonging to human nature. It should be underlined, that this pattern of understanding that honors the important, perhaps *the most important* role of a newly understood notion of wholeness is embedded in what R. M. Unger called in his 2007 study on *The Self Awakened* an "accelerating change".[7] Each linear and intuitive understanding of history, separated form the notion of wholeness, is in that perspective an obstacle to understand the structure of our future and the shift of paradigms in a hitherto unimagined pace.

5.1.2 Jurisprudential Involvements

The 'how' and 'why' of the term 'conversion jurisprudence' is essential in this Brief. *Conversion* existed long before the introduction of the digital culture and technique. Today, the term belongs to both types of language. Both are in effect as conversions of material fragments (for instance of molecular up to atomic and subatomic structures) but also as an important sector in telecommunication, which converts codes and units, even commands and data that broaden and perfect communication on a global scale. Energy conversion is for instance important in the general study and several specific solution attempts of climate change problems.

The accelerating rate of change has been a scientific issue for already a decade, but it did not lead to a reliable extension of theoretical insight in the flow of human knowledge. The transition from analog to digital insights and the view on the phenomenon of time as a non-linear and exponential phenomenon did not lead to a deeper insight of conversion as the power behind those changes. The higher rates of paradigm shifts and the fast growth of information technologies as well as global expansion of connectivity are able to emulate human intelligence. But they did hitherto not lead to deeper insight in conversion. New mental models of reality and human intelligence became possible. "With it, the position of the extreme non-naïve-natural, which is in development versus a point of transcendence, would become newly understood and defined. It would introduce as truly twenty-first century philosophy."[8] The latter, we underline, is not possible without the theme of conversion.

Conversion of meaning and use is mostly related to speaking and writing, for short: to various types of direct linguistic activity. In other words: conversion must

---

[7]Unger (2007, 6).

[8]Broekman (2010, 74).

be understood as a newly discovered aspect of language. That is relevant for law and its discourses. All words spoken and heard are not only at the *level of reception*, as the digital culture problematically accentuates, but at the very same time the *level of reaction*. 'Reception' and 'reaction' are components of conversion. Hermeneutics share this view; texts interpretations become effective only through recognition of these dynamics. Converting components of language quicken our movements inwards—they turn us to our Wholeness, of which we think to have lost all contact with. That Wholeness was in Kantian words as well as in Husserl's formulations a *transcendental* substance that marks conversions. What does it mean for law?

5.1.3 Conversion Involvements

Conversions between words, texts or fragments of text, speech and meanings, occur in law's languages as wholes. But the fundamental structure of conversion remains throughout comparable: a comparison between different sets or complexities of convertible units is in essence a comparison between specific wholes. It should thus be underlined what was already described in the above paragraphs: *the concepts of conversion and wholeness are closely linked.* Not the importance or correctness of this observation, but the specific qualities in effect have to be studied when jurisprudence is submitted to a process of rethinking.

Any conversion depends on *the situation and the purpose concerned.* The case of conversion jurisprudence is clearly profiled in that regard. Modern law desires actuality and accuracy of insight and conversion, key concept in answering this situation, is the purpose that requires enlightenment. Word/text units appearing in law and legal sciences as well as the relevant historical definitions and qualifications (such as 'prose', 'poetry', 'code', 'law') require an accuracy of measurement of the conversion. The latter touches the heart of legal language. But accuracy is difficult to confirm. Legal prose has therefore created its own rules, which are institutionally safeguarded. It is understood as an artificial language and is thanks to this form of understanding more controllable in cases of comparison and thus of conversion.

5.1.4 ADC and DAC Involvements

That remains also the case in the center of digital expressivity and its conversional operations. The most well-known and widely studied conversions are therefore the *Analog-Digital Converter (ADC)* as well as the *Digital-Analog Converter (DAC)* in the complexity of analog/digital language. Both are outstanding member of the globally extended family of converters. All converters play a dominant role in the ever-changing world of today—but how should we differentiate them? Converters are everywhere; they belong to fields of sciences as well as the occurrences of our ordinary daily life. Everything changes and is brought to change: converters perform what occurs anyway, one could say. They really form a transcendental reality in modern life.

The DAC and the ADC have common features: they are important in lingual expressivity; they are a specific type of conversion and in parallel a type of language; they are set free by 'digital technologies'. But new is the fact that a DAC strictly functioning in digital settings differs from a DAC functioning in linguistic (mixed analog and digital) contexts. Language has transcendental features, is not a matter of exact measuring and is not determined by a strict program of performance. Its transcendental character is represented by the way we can understand DAC as a cloud (a well-known digital term) and not as a strict series of rules to apply.

The DAC, the digital-to-analog convertor, is the twin brother of the ADC, the analog-digital convertor. This twining should never be forgotten; it characterizes the conversion process in all regards. The ADC is generally known and used as the conversion, which is necessary for the actually expanding *datafication process* that plays the major role in the solving of scientific and everyday-life problems. Datafication should for that reason be studied as a social force, which characterizes modern culture and is based on the omnipresence of the ADC. The latter in its turn proves the omnipresence of the digital in analog patterns of thought in everyday life. Consulting our smart phone without an effective ADC in context would be unthinkable.

The latter observation illustrates also, how dependent any *datafication* process is on the DAC, the electronic circuit that converts digital data into analog signals. One has the feeling that what was digitalized in life, should come back to us in analog form. That feeling is a strange feeling. Does it suggest that the analog language and its spheres of expressivity is our natural context, and the digital an incidental, temporarily and technical means of life that should safeguard its artificial character? Reformulate that question: if we keep every component of our contemporary life in analog context, we risk to be appreciated as "old-fashioned". If, on the other hand, we succeed to keep all components of life in a digital context, we are "techno-pirates", a "tech head" or perhaps a "computer whiz". Who decides what and why? Cyberlaw unfolds amidst these considerations. It is attracted by the virtues and techniques of the digital culture, depends importantly on *datafication*, but needs to listen and interpret DAC results carefully. Those who read law are generally confronted with DAC results, seldom with issues concerning the ADC functions. Any consideration focusing on the DAC has to unfold in the heart of the digital thought patterns and their world. An analog type of language, technique and thought formation, one concludes, is always nearby and fulfills life in all regards, those of digital nature included. That inclusion brings us to the DAC's importance: the riddle of its *conversion* abilities and techniques. The most important specification of a DAC is *its precise resolution*. That resolution is, in contrast to the analog twin brother ADC, the way in which (for instance by the numbers of its bits) the device can be defined.

The DAC is thus indispensible for all global digital technicalities and the world-wide economics of digital devices. Computers only recognize digital information, so that their in- and output is always connected to digital formats/types of language.

But some devices realizing output will only accept analog input. The use of a digital-to-analog converter, or DAC, is thus needed in all cases of any use of whatever type of computer. As suggested, the numbers of its bits or its step sizes, define a DAC resolution. But why do we need data converters? The answer is relatively simple: in the real world, most data are available in the form of what is indicated in analog expressivity as "nature". While manipulating data, the two converting interfaces of the AD and the DA are essential to digital electronic equipment *plus* an analog device. The "plus" is surprisingly important. The goal of the digital equipment is to measure, filter or compress real-world analog signals. *All data ultimately require conversion to an analog signal in order to interact with the real world.* Not only in the electronic world, but also in the world of our daily speech is this differentiation between analog and digital language essential. Speech and electronics seem in that regard parallel events of everyday.

Like in the world of electronics, is in the world of language and speech a conversion between the two types of language (via ADC and DAC) essential. The point is, there exist multiple electronic devices for DA conversion in general but there is no instrument—not even a dictionary—that can be considered as a device for *specifically linguistic* DA conversions. This failing balance between ordinary speech and a correlative use of electronics does not inspire a theory or philosophy of language to consider the issue more profoundly! Emphasis is on the specificities of digital communication, which became familiar in today's social media. They created a new digital landscape in human communication. The question whether the digital character of such a landscape fulfills the central question of communication: "to reach out to the other", is not posed. Who is "the other", what is "communication" in digital worlds?

Focus on the DAC underlines that converters have in general *many tools* available. Some are determinative, whereas others are excluded from *linguistic DAC activities*. Since there does not exist a systematic theory of the DAC in general, one has to search for traces of the DAC structure in the multiple conversions—a research project that became hitherto not realized. The many DAC tools are accompanied by many and various techniques, which show a specific and characteristic pattern. But the fact remains, that *differences* in the DAC structure related to language are difficult to sum up. First, the *streaming of electricity*, which is a basic phenomenon in the DAC (even in the case of changing output voltages), cannot be completely compared to the *streaming of meaning and sense* of linguistic elements, which is basic for language in general and speech in particular. Secondly, the same is true for the *streaming of sound*, which is inherent to speech (cf. the difference between noise and sound). And thirdly is the function and meaning of *significance* too different to function well in a comparison with the DAC's digital basis. So, why and how would one try to grasp the effects of the DAC in the context of digital conversation? Several aspects seem to be important in this context:

- The question comes up because of the profound relationship between digital conversation on the one hand and the double definition of a word in language on the other. The third decade of the 21st century opens with the global experience that no word of an analog language type exists and functions without its digital counterpart, and vice versa. It is clear that this observation is of utmost importance for law and legal practice, and via this relationship is the DAC important for legal thought formation.

- This *new binary compound* fascinates so powerfully that the function of *conversions* between the two linguistic levels and their mutual influences concerning meaning and sense appears to be minimized. The effects of the two conversions, the ADC and the DAC, are nevertheless important: they master and manage analog speech and digital expressivity at their specific singular level as well as in their level of intertwining. Legal language cannot distance itself from this binary structure.
- To suggest that a specific *conversion* can be decisive in qualitative forms of digital conversation does *not* imply that any conclusion about this conversion activity (humanly performed or machine-made) is independent and categorized as a single cause. On the contrary: here is again an *intertwining* of meanings and constitutive powers, among which for instance *emotions* play an important role. The latter emphasizes the importance of researching this topic as well as its ties with legal thoughts.
- Consider the DAC conversion as a "*soft conversion*". This does not include the necessity (or even the technical opportunity laid down in the conversion flow) to change the items' configuration. It means that no increase or decrease of the precision of measures is guaranteed. All factors at stake in a soft conversion are understood and interpreted as belonging to engineering judgments. In the DAC functioning in linguistic contexts, the precision is in the mutual understanding of the (spoken) word. The embedding of the spoken word in such mutual structures is typical for legal language and law's practices based on that (partially artificial) type of language. The speakers involved in that process are considered to be free—they are as free as a speaker is free, or in digital terms: a sender is free: to perform. The freedom in soft conversion includes learning (acquisition and rules for using information), reasoning (rules to come to conclusions) and self-correction.

5.1.5 To Articulate Conversion

The soft conversion may at the end be a relevant step towards understanding language, and in particular a text, as *a narrative sequence of events, which is fundamentally open to digital understanding*. The question whether computers understand the text they bring to the fore might be less important than the question what effects the software environment has available for broadening the patterns of our understanding beyond the 'naked eye'. In particular the linguistically relevant type of DAC might open new ways to explore our narrative impulses. The latter are more and more understood as a technique to unfold what meanings are sustained by our actual insight in today's dual typology of language in the multiple levels of communication. This determines our insights and our practices about the multiple language modalities we are confronted with in law and life.

But there is more to consider. Are meanings separate and independent language components in this context? Within the framework of conversion a certain threat must be signaled, which changes law and legal discourse fundamentally: to speak in law might become the same as sending a message under the influence of the combination between conversion and digitalization. That type of message will remain in essence linguistic but change in the forthcoming years into no more than a specifically prepared data, fabricated by legal computer programs. The latter are already imaginable in special legal sectors (such as economics, contracts, certain domains of criminal behavior, laws regulating traffic on the street as well as on the Internet) but are not fully available yet to fill and dominate the entire province of law and legal discourse. This description indicates actual changes in law based on the relation between our thinking legal thoughts and the processes we named 'conversion'. But the latter is broader and deeper than the first. To think conversion and law as one of its ever-changing domains is not the same as thinking language.

Semioticians already warned us that legal signs could be transferred and communicated linguistically although they are in essence not identical with language! A philosophy of signs, being the heart of semiotics, is not identical with a philosophy of language. And a philosophy of conversion (for instance pertaining to law) is also not identical with a philosophy of language. Where conversion occurs is language one of the major instruments to grasp its meaning and sense, but it is not identical with it! In other words: *conversion encompasses language despite the fact that language can be an instrument to understand and even profile conversion*. For that reason is the originally digital concept 'conversion' much broader and more encompassing than for instance DAC conversion techniques. So we suggested the term 'soft conversion' as characteristic for *lingual* conversions. The softness implies a distance to a purely mechanical and instrumental understanding of our rethinking in the shadows of conversion processes. In the case of law does this attitude distance the legal professional from the linguistically important Speaker-Hearer Model, but also from his self-understanding as a unique legal subject that is untouchable by conversion. This is why and how legal thoughts convert, one concludes!

Conversion was studied in the context of a large cultural pattern, as the Occidental culture shows. Components of conversion are today always linked with components of digital culture and techniques. Today are all conversions embedded in well-trusted foundational ideas and options of a culture, which are in a process of globalizing; but they will at the same time be automated. The digital culture and its technicality attempt to transcend philosophical and other foundational ideas. It means that our latest technology seeks to strive for more powerful tools to process information. It evolves therefore necessarily on a global scale, because this technique distances itself in theory and practice from social values of states or groups of states and their respective cultures. This might change law's discourse and its purposes in a more radical way than we could ever think of when the first appearances of digital thoughts and techniques unfolded.

5.1.6 Socio-Ethical Involvements

There is an important aspect to underline. All conversions influenced by digital techniques and fragments of culture that belong to the language(s) of law, share basic values and thoughts that are common to the variety of global cultures. They are always composed by ideas that transcend boundaries, such as the limits of racial profiles or other specific traditions in human life (among which individualism). And they keep these profiles and values intact. They concern values like 'speaking a language', 'accepting scientific and/or philosophical standards', 'appreciating basic ideas like "wholeness", "partition", "causality" or "not to be rebuttable"' and the like. Those values beyond which one cannot think, judge or imagine a human life are also beyond anyone's personal judgment or ethical positioning. In this context must be underlined, that conversions seem in general non-individualized powers or systems that accept forms of individualization.

That characteristic remains a major determination in the case of values or normative systems, which constitute law's practices through conversions. Today's attempts to transcend the boundaries of digital insights via DAC's or through manipulation of ADC's, create a profile for the future that seems indescribable in analog or digital terms. The two do not possess the quality to describe that future. They are directly (analog) and indirectly (digital) individualistic and directed resp. dependent upon particular and detectable parts that fulfill a role in profiling, utterance and research. In the language of a future technology one can for instance no longer use words such as 'wholeness' or 'conversion' as individualized components or particles of thought patterns, let alone maintain the concept of 'jurisprudence'!

That takes us to the true tasks of rethinking law and legal thought formation. As we mentioned in Chap. 3 of this Brief, Marx was very near to describing this problem. He focused on the changes in France's political and social structure during the days of Napoleon Bonaparte's *coup d'état*. But Proudhon was characterized as an "objective historian" who reconstructed events as basically individualistic, and Marx criticized Hugo because the latter judged Napoleon's deeds as "the violent act of a single individual". It is clear: any cloud of conversion is not explained nor sustained by individualistic approaches. Marx' search for an existential understanding of master-conversions that rein our lives reaches further than any of his theories or his globally known and disputed social philosophy could indicate. That observation is of utmost importance, because we stated that there is no law or legal discourse without conversion. The question arises: what about the individualistic features characterizing law?

5.2 Converting Conversions Convert

The influence of a mother tongue on personal and social dimensions of linguistic articulation seems limited if one considers the actual developments in Western Europe—especially because comparable evolutions take place in other regions of the world. These evolutions show many *multi*cultural ways of life and there are many *multi*lingual speakers around, so that daily life is often a matter of placing oneself and the other in an adequate context—a task not unknown to a legal professional and his program. It means that *translations/conversions* posses nowadays a form of naturalness, which equals a mother tongue. A spoken word needs not only a speaker but also a context; it needs another individual as hearer, but also a common world of life-patterns and their specific expressivity.

5.2.1 No Law Without Conversion

This is an interesting challenge for the practices of legal functionaries, in particular those who are confronted with digital/analog and analog/digital languages, e.g. judges or lawyers. They are, as we formulated in the above paragraph, decidedly influenced by the fact that a conversion is never a single, well defined, fixated and sealed fact, form or energy that functions as the cause of conversions. They connect, on the contrary, always with an energy that is also in conversion activity itself. The flow, streaming and multiplicity, the multileveled character and the being-a-cloud in itself (the *substantive*) characterizes and enforces each phase of conversion in time and space (the *verb*).

We question with an eye on the legal professional whether conversions sustain law's individualistic features. It seems necessary, because it could surprise those who read law: the conversions that are converting from natural- towards legal language are converting in themselves during their conversion activity! This is the unexpected and often surprising feature of conversion as a mark of jurisprudence. If the practices of jurists all around are influenced by the fact that a conversion is never a single, well defined, fixated and sealed fact, or an operation with such facts, which functions as the cause of conversions (conversion as *verb*), then conversions are in essence neither individualistic nor collectivistic.

Ask an investigating judge, a criminal judge, a specialist in international contracts or a family law attorney what conversion structures he or she has to apply. Ask him or her in the natural language both of you share. But an answer is difficult: "what is the *subject* of your thoughts in this case?" will be answered in terms that refer to a *legal* subjectivity. You have to understand and practice law to decipher the answer even if it is formulated in a natural language. The *legal* subject is not 'my daughter' or 'your grandfather', nor the stocks and shares they posses or for instance their responsibility in the case of an accident. The subject in law is the product of a conversion pertaining to all those possible nominations. A conversion from naïve-natural to artificial language, which creates individualistic traits as a major property of law, is probably the simplest clause to propose. And, one has to add, that legal individualism is a matter of legal construction provoking the fulfillment of cultural requirements. An example is in the fact that law's discourse created its own first person singular, which could refer to an ownership of rights and duties. The riddle of *alter*'s presence seems at issue when natural language becomes converted into legal language. This conversion activity was in the beginning of the 20th century named 'fiction', and should perhaps be renamed in the context of understanding jurisprudence as a deeply anchored conversion process.

5.2.2 Conversions Convert

If conversions convert (e.g. legal thoughts) they do so while in the meantime converting in themselves, and not as a fixated entity apart from what they convert (e.g. legal thoughts). In other words: when conversions convert, do they already convert in themselves. Do not forget: each tongue generates and articulates a world-view, a narrative of human destiny, a construct of futurities for which there is no facsimile in any other. In other words: each tongue refers to what constitutes its wholeness—and by the act of this reference, creates a specific wholeness. The latter is active when *conversion* brings all those ideas together and thus appears to be a key in understanding language—and our self, perhaps even our self as a legal subject!

This Brief focuses on a broader and more risky reflection. As was noticed before: there is no jurist today whose words are not embedded in analog *and* in digital connotations—no matter what type or form of meaning is concerned. This fact becomes clear in the terms and concepts the legal professional tends to study and apply. Hermeneutics illustrates the meanings of legal expressivity in an extensive manner. The terms and their meaning-precision does indeed seem a matter of walking thin lines between fact and fiction. But, as was suggested during our entire rethinking process: those occurrences are altogether embedded in conversions. One specific property of these conversions should, however, not become systematized in a traditional logical and scientific manner: conversions convert their own meaning and sense during their own and immediate conversion activity (i.e. without mediation). We conclude: changes represented by conversions are never fixated, detectable and stabilized, but they change with their changes. They are for that reason compared with *clouds* and never with *fixated* or *stabilized* issues. We therefore ventured the thesis that conversion is broader and fundamentally different from language: a movement of culture and with it of human essence and its foundational forms of humanity.

This insight causes us to reach beyond traditional borderlines. When jurists are aware how their legal language is a matter of plural types of language embracing more than one type of cultural domain, then they are also observing *the horizon of their expressivity*. At that horizon, or perhaps hardly visibly upcoming beyond it, might be linguistic and scientific phenomena that once will be completely above the horizon and will change what occurs at this moment. This possibility is one of the most powerful motives to repeatedly refer to concepts that relate to conversions and their activities of creating meaning and sense. There is no thinking that is free from the multiplicity of determinative factors in the meaning concept and free from the idea to originate in a human knowledge based on partitioning and fixation of meaning-particles. But it remains of importance, that words can only *after* an exodus from meaninglessness (think of Husserl's 'naïve-natural attitude) become a prevailing component and a layer of meaning in human existence, and through this existence of any importance in cosmic occurrences. It seems worthwhile to consider that a meaningful articulation is not solely a human process, but that it has implications via human language in which humans share their destiny with meanings amidst unknown presences of signifiers in the cosmos.

Thanks to a globally intensified communication and its digital connectivity techniques became conversion a key-activity in nearly all fields of thoughts, sciences and social life. It is absolutely no exception to mention jurisprudence as a field influenced by its problems, insights, forces and requirements. Money, measures or weights are to be converted, but also words, insights and opinions, let alone judgments and provisions. Conversion is part of the moving of the world of everyday and so it touches all our lives, their legal dimensions included. As a consequence, conversion intrudes everybody's existence everywhere—not only in professional roles but also in a majority of private aspects of life. Facts offered in real life situations are nearly always embedded in the mainstream of conversions. Yet, there is a difference between the omnipresence of digital communication and the presence of conversion powers. The first is like a cloud over our daily life and its entire cultural sphere, which surveys everyone everywhere. The latter has a history that is traceable and thus understandable differently: not only a consequence of technical innovations and changes, but seemingly anchored in social life. That anchor might profile the riddle of conversion.

5.2.3 Soft Conversion

An argument in favor of bringing conversion and jurisprudence together is in essence a linguistic justification. Each tongue generates and articulates a world-view, as does each juridical position. Law and language come closely together when utterances, which we call speech-events, take place. The narrative of humanity and its destiny is determined by what seems to be meaning-transition. They construct the narrative called 'future' as they did construct the narrative called 'past'. The two are moments of a wholeness that characterizes and supports conversion. Conversion is the word that indicates the continuous flow of life in both: in landscape as well as in time. However, one should cautiously focus on the specificity of the conversion that will be proposed as adjective for the rethought form of law called jurisprudence. There are many modes of conversion in various fields of science, technology and social studies. Some lead from one level to another, for instance when there has to be conversed either in Analog or Digital type of language, or back again. These cause a more encompassing interest in conversion, which is in itself differentiated between types of language at various levels. *Meaning* is always involved in the main outline of those differences, which make conversion necessary.

Conversion of units occurs in sciences and engineering through multiplicative factors. However, this might be different when conversion between words (resp. of texts or fragments of text, let alone speech fragments, their references to meanings included) is concerned. In cases of conversion one has to notice that the relevant fundamental structure remains throughout a comparison. Comparing between different sets or complexities of convertible units is in essence a comparison between specific wholes. It should be underlined for this reason what was already outlined: *the concepts of conversion and wholeness are closely linked.* Not the importance or truth of this observation, but the specific qualities in effect have to be studied when jurisprudence is submitted to a process of rethinking. With these words is also confirmed that a conversion depends on the situation and the purpose in general. The case of conversion jurisprudence is clearly profiled with these considerations. Modern law desires actuality of insight, and conversion is, as a key concept in understanding the situation, a final purpose.

Rethinking focuses on the qualities of conversion in the case of law: the riddle of application of laws, of appropriateness of legal rules, the implications of justice maintained in judgments, decisions pertaining to legal qualification or even the often sarcastically understood notions of diction and fiction in legal language are altogether issues of conversion. It is surprising, how law's hermeneutics seems to be resurrected and many issues regarding law's appreciation on the street no longer a matter of social conflict only.

Rethinking legal thought formation seems worthwhile! It includes a unique awareness about how conversions convert—the crux of this Brief! Conversions convert while converting themselves, without awareness of the identity changes caused by the process—often even without indicating any identity that will become registered in human knowledge. There is no alphabetically order that determines their effect in life. There is no chain of digits that fulfills such a function. Conversions seem to operate beyond our guesses and attempts to find any orderly scheme for their activity. Their influence on meaning and sense in social life as well as in human individual existence seems broader than our intelligence. So, are conversions a matter of disorder, non-logical patterning or a mastering of post-intelligible meaning? There would be a most remarkable parallel with authoritarian views on law and State, like Hobbes developed, if one accepts that conclusion. In that case would the Power of Conversion parallel the Power of the *Leviathan*. And, be not afraid to conclude: both are *humanized* in that parallel. The latter seems a secret formative power in social effect.

Is that correct?

It is, but the philosophical implications are difficult to understand, let alone to master in thought processes to which law and legal discourse belong. The broadening of our ability to grasp the fragments of reality, which unfold before our eyes leads to dimensions that are normally not linked with law or other disciplines concerning human social behavior. Conversions are ultimately not a matter of changes in meaning, replacements or translations, transferences of substance or even a *metanoia*—they concern the sense (or the senses) of existence: terrestrial, global, even cosmic. Tensions between *meaning* and *sense* dominate them. Are these not classical tensions? In any case, they refer to broader and more encompassing views on conversion and the unfolding human life in its cosmic context.

Conversions embrace hitherto unformulated philosophical issues. Thoughts and experiments reaching beyond boundaries of traditional means of expression bring to the fore that processes in natural reality are outreaching wider and broader, deeper and different in time and energy than human knowledge can articulate, embrace and express. Law illustrates how there is no object of human knowledge that is fully known and articulated by a human mind. The idea that there exists a parallel or even a perhaps hidden identity between human knowledge and fragments of nature's status seems incorrect. It thus becomes disputable to treat entities like 'wholeness' as completed and independent empirical parts of human knowledge and thus as meaningful terms of one's power to express. Philosophical terms and concepts are often debatable because of these tendencies towards a dangerously naïve generalization. The character of what is named '*soft conversion*' does not annihilate this danger; it should also not conceal the problems of human perception and experience related to conversion in law and life.

5.3 A Conversation

One of the many sunny afternoons in September 2019 shows us *Phil*, jurist, *Jack*, IT-er and *August*, philosophy teacher, walking the backyard of College Park. All three did read this Brief. Phil looks disquieted, Jack dissatisfied, and August, curious about their attitude, tries to communicate, saying: "Why"?

They walk around and then take a seat at a small terrace. Phil considers how to answer the "why" when Jack bursts out: " … because it all looked so promising. I understand, and accept to be engaged in processes of conversion. Many days I just do that job: trying to master conversions between analog and digital fragments of our life today".

A smile of August accompanies signs of impatience on Phil's face.

But Jack adds hastily: "I experience how changes take place, how the digital becomes more and more important in the lives of people. Look at their *gaming* passions, look at Apple and others—the gaming is in fact not technically but financially interesting, no matter whether it is socially catastrophic or not." After a few seconds he completes: "But here you are: conversions, even those in process of converting themselves, do not tell me where we go or what will be the result of the impressive moves of our AI–provided new algorithms. What are we doing? Do we do what they tell us to do most intelligently—embracing our mathematical intelligence? Are they our Modern Masters?"

Phil remarks grinning: "But, you are in a powerful position, Jack! I experience more uncertainty, which I cannot tell my client. The limits of my knowledge and the boundaries of exploring what is known and what seems unknowable may in part still be understood in terms of law and legal value orientation. Legal informatics and cyberlaw illustrate an attempt to also create such an understanding in contact with digital knowledge. Many legal contracts, judgments, decisions or opinions are often based on the presupposition that the situation on which law reacts, is known or is in principle knowable. 'Investigation' is for that reason an almost sacred term in most branches of law. But do I have to reflect on the relation between 'investigation' and 'conversion'? Don't laugh: the latter will devour the first!"

Jack interrupts, and asks Phil whether he is disappointed not to have algorithms at his disposal. Phil sights: "Does the lawyer, the judge or even the social worker have any guarantee that he or she fully *knows* the situation that requires his action prescribed in law's discourses and texts?" Half a minute later, we hear him say: "Or is that knowledge just a socially accepted presupposition, which is true and untrue at the same time, or in a word cherished by modernity: a fake?"

August wants to find common ground, and remarks: "Scientific and technological research like digital or quantum technologies embrace a specific goal. Their scientists are for instance not interested in the behavior of sub-atomic particles as such, but they study those levels because they are driven by a particular desire: they want to perfect information and thus change communication. All scientific and technological research—language, culture, basic units or particles—embraces that goal. It leads to creating information in ways that reach beyond our alphabets, chains of bits or series of apps."

Phil sights: "And it will deliver programs that automate law and do not solve my unique legal problems. It will change law and legal discourse in manners, which create priority for the program rather than for law as a force that entangles social problems. The traditional model that focuses on a speaker and a hearer remains at a great distance. Yes, you're right, those two are far away, as if it were an ethnographic issue with little substance and interest today. It also indicates a definitive loss of value-orientated or ethical dimensions belonging to the image of man in law anymore. That's what worries me."

Jack asks aggressively: "Do you mean, the price for perfect information, communicated better than ever, is too high: the price is the annihilation or a conversion of values and ethical attitude? But do you know any substance, which remains untouched by conversions?"

August tries to intermediate: "Computer programs do perhaps open ways for a more perfect and newly automated relation between lawyer and client. They focus on an inter-human reality, which neither digital nor quantum technology is able to formulate or to adequately articulate. The DAC has proven this. The gap is deep; the perfection of newly developed and totally differently operating computers is not able to bridge that lacuna. But it makes the lawyer think about the virtues of conversion with new forms and phenomena at the horizon. Don't forget: the future legal and political system will be composed of the Web and the Big Data!"

Phil wants to show how he supports August: "Rethinking law and its thought patterns including the forces, structures and processes of legal conversion, should in the first place clarify the specific position of their own activity. Is conversion not a newly discovered phenomenon in my discipline? Today are new forms of information and communication a phenomenon at the horizon—but for how long, nobody can say. If information becomes the only central and multi-layered concept in my discipline, it will be delivered as independent from a subject in distress and submitted to new forms of processing, constructing and transmitting of data".

He adds vehemently: "That should justify the distance a lawyer and his or her client has acquired between the need and the provision of law! Shit, that really makes me shiver."

August reacts immediately. "Yes, you are right—but there is more to say, especially to you, jurist, lawyer, judge, legal specialist! Information is a central and multi-layered concept. It is on its way to be delivered as independent from an informing/interpreting subject and submitted to new forms of processing and transmission of data. The US philosopher Charles S. Peirce could in his days not imagine how important his urge to understand the qualities of an *interpretant* was. And they still are! Today's digital culture delivers already information via streams of bits that are pulses representing a zero or one. Forthcoming computers will work with conversion as an absolute force and will thus be *transformative* instead of *informative*. The first devours the latter, Phil!"

Looking at Jack, August adds: "The quality of your algorithm cannot bridge the gap, Jack—your refined information will show its face. Conversions embedding new approaches so deeply in social life use names as playing cards; the card called information will not inform but transform!"

Phil rises from his chair. It is as if he wants to walk away, but he suddenly stands next to Jack and looks over his shoulder: "My discipline is one of words, Jack. And its innermost purpose is a great value: justice. Your professional moves from words to digits and from there perhaps to quats disregard the value of that value! And the value of a value in general! Your discipline operates with time likewise: mine measures the days and hours of a human life, yours will one day step over thousands of years being a time unit observed in- and transferred from subatomic to socio-political levels, as Apple boasted these days according to the Sept 2019 *Financial Times* reports. Do you have in mind what those conversions mean in the history of mankind?"

August feels Phil's anger, and intervenes: "Phil will tell you how your activity might cause, that there is no '*wholeness*' anymore in our rethinking, but only a '*totality*' named to be a surpassing phase of knowledge."

Phil adds hastily: "And there will be no '*values*' anymore, neither in law nor in aesthetics, but '*attitudes*' instead. These will be said to express *the essence of man* in law and society. They will be clarified in non-social terms, which create domains of automatism and absolutism. That development might even no longer recognize what today is called a 'human individual'. In your perspective, law will disappear and become a social automatism. No justice anymore, only equilibrium!" He walks back to his chair.

August completes what was said to Jack: "Phil expressed, that a major concern of law and legal discourse appears to be (in the light of developments in your discipline) a matter of *re-humanization* of life and social togetherness. Conversions show their changes through changing the meanings of words! With it, an deep *differentiation* of types of human lives and human features might become a precious social attitude again."

"The tendencies of technical foundations inherent to actual conversions seem very forceful indeed. They could create a globe with a humanity that finds its purpose in an equality of lifestyle, knowledge and experience. We, in the IT–discipline and technology, are not critical in that regard. Our technological drive does not take values, norms and comparable qualities as an issue separated from ongoing developments," Jack attempted to remark.

But the three want to leave the Park; the sun is already going down. August tries to conclude: "We read the Brief. The text made clear how the psychic *emptiness* of the modern '*homo sapiens*' could inspire a new drive to unfold life. It has to unfold in hands, which are now filled with smart phones. And so are the minds: filled with material and psychical features delivered by computer programs. They will at some time in future be pictured as one of the many evolutionary phases of humanity. But mind you, friends, *humanization* is a feature beyond such unfolding patterns in sciences and philosophy. Why…"

He looks around in the Park.

No horizon: only bushes and buildings.

References

Broekman, J. M. (2010). Firstness and phenomenology—Peirce and Husserl on attitude change. In A. Wagner & J. M. Broekman (Eds.), (2010, 2012) *Prospects of legal semiotics* (pp. 37–79). Dordrecht, Heidelberg, London, New York: Springer.

Husserl, E. (1954). Die Krisis der Europäischen Wissenschaften und die Transzendentale Phänomenologie (1935/37). In W. Biemel (Ed.). Den Haag, The Netherlands: Martinus Nijhoff.

Husserl, E. (1956). Erste Philosophie (1923/24), Erster Teil: Kritische Ideengeschichte. In R. Boehm (Ed.). Den Haag, The Netherlands: Martinus Nijhoff.

Husserl, E. (1959). Erste Philosophie (1923/24). Zweiter Teil: Theorie der phänomenologischen Reduktion. In R. Boehm (Ed.). Den Haag, The Netherlands: Martinus Nijhoff.

Kant, I. (1781 [Ed. A], 1787 [Ed. B]). *Kritik der reinen Vernunft*. In J. F. Hartknoch, Riga, Dld.

Unger, R. M. (2007). *The self awakened*. Cambridge, MA: Harvard University Press.